To Karen,

I hope this [barcode] you

get through zing

times.

Author Your Life,

David

In Memory of Jim McCrae
(21/07/1939-24/07/2015)

Contents

<u>Prologue</u>

<u>**16:00, Friday 24th July, 2015**</u>

"What a horrible place to come to die," I remarked.

I was walking through the hospice in my hometown. An old hospital, half of the site had fallen into dilapidation, it looked like walking through an apocalyptic landscape or a horror movie.

My girlfriend squeezed my hand in response, as I reorientated my focus towards the site that was maintained; small lodge-like buildings and neat flowerbeds and hedges presented a much nicer scene. Small comfort in the current situation.

Eight months previously, on Christmas Eve 2014, my Dad had been diagnosed with terminal cancer of the lungs and liver, and given 6-8 months to live. My dad had waited until May 27th 2015 to tell me, when I had finished my last exams at university. Just when I thought I was on top of the world and ready for an exciting new adventure, I found out that I was going to lose my Dad at age 22.

In the month or so after this revelation, I took it in my stride to try and maximise what time we had left. I interviewed Dad about his life, wrote him a gratitude letter thanking him for everything he had done for me, and visited him to show him pictures and videos of my graduation (Dad was too weak to travel by this point). Around the time of my graduation, Dad developed jaundice as his liver began to fail to break down the toxins in his body, and in mid-July he was admitted to Aberdeen hospital in Scotland.

When I visited Dad in hospital, I was shocked at how weak he had become. Dad was a feisty, vibrant character, always cracking jokes and entertaining people with his stories and opinions. However, when I saw him in the hospital bed he was faint and low, both in his conduct and his spiritual energy. The doctors wanted to do an operation to try and clear the toxins from his bile duct. I realised that if they weren't successful, then my Dad didn't have long to live.

A week later, on the 23rd of July, they tried to do the operation, but upon closer examination they declared the cancer was too far spread for them to do anything, and Dad was now entering his final days. He was going to be moved from hospital to hospice care. I received the call telling me this midway through the day.

Whilst I had had the time to prepare myself mentally for this eventuality, nothing truly prepares you for when that phone call comes through. I was in a daze as I called my girlfriend to tell her. By coincidence she was heading back to our hometown in Aberdeenshire the following day (we lived in Glasgow, three hours away from our hometown and my Dad). I booked a train ticket to travel up with her.

I'm so thankful things turned out the way they did. There was a lack of urgency about my desire to return to Dad. I was too shocked to think properly. I guess I had this romantic image of sitting by his bedside over the weekend, chatting, reading stories, watching him sleep, all the things that happened in the movies. I don't know whether it was ignorance or denial that kept me jumping on a train right away.

We caught our train at noon, and we were up in our hometown just after three. I found a card to write for Dad in my girlfriend's house, and took the time to sign it from all my close friends (time David!).

So I found myself walking through the ruins of the old hospital at four pm, and was relying upon black humour to occupy my mind as we walked. Me and Dad had joked about his upcoming death a lot, both of us had a philosophical and spiritual view on death, so we did not fear it (although it does become a little more daunting when it turns from a philosophical to practical discussion!). I also won't deny that it was a coping strategy, and trying to keep joy and humour, benchmarks of our relationship, intact as long as we could.

I entered the main entrance, I had texted ahead to let the family know I was coming, and I was surprised to see about half a dozen of them waiting for me in the reception. My aunt, and my nieces and nephews from my half-sisters. They all greeted me warmly and said they were so glad I was here.

"We were worried you wouldn't make it," one of my nieces said to me.

Worried I wouldn't make it? I was coming to a romantic weekend wasn't I? Sitting by Dad's bedside and chatting about life until he gently passed. Suddenly I was aware that might not be the way it was going to turn out.

"Just to warn you, he's quite bad, are you okay?" They saw that this was sinking in for me.

"Yes," I summoned my courage, "let's do this."

My family lead me and my girlfriend through the hospice. I will always remember the room number, 26, same as the day I was born. I entered that room at about 4:15pm.

We pulled back the curtain, and there was my Dad. His skin was yellow from the jaundice. His bed-shirt was open on one shoulder, exposing his gaunt collarbones: Dad had lost 4 stone (25kg) in the course of his cancer. He was groaning in pain and my half-sister held a cup under his mouth in case he was sick. A few more members of the family, cousins, were in the room.

I hadn't prepared myself for this. I rushed to the side of his bed and grabbed his limp, frail hand as everyone proclaimed: "Look David's here."

"I'm here Dad. I'm here," I confirmed, the fear rising in me.

"Are the painkillers kicking in Dad?" my half-sister asked.

"Marginally." My Dad's voice was barely audible, a croak.

"We'll leave the two of you together," someone said.

Everyone left the room, as they did, my half-sister whispered in my ear: "He's been holding on for you David."

Suddenly I was hit with how important this moment was. I knew this was going to be my last opportunity to speak to Dad. There weren't going to be romantic conversations over the next couple of days. Whatever needed to be said, needed to be said.

I didn't have a script for this situation, so I admit I somewhat rambled. The first point I managed to kind of articulate was that I was going to be all right. I told him I had things planned for the business; I told him that I'd sorted out a new flat; I'd told him my relationship was going well; I told him I knew what I was doing; that he'd prepared me well; and I was ready to go on without him. After this rambling I started to hone in on what was important. What did I need to tell him right now? In that moment, with Dad's death imminent, I hit on three of the most important things I will ever say.

"Thank you for the fantastic job you did of raising me; I'm incredibly proud to be your son; I love you Dad."

That was the first time I had ever said the words "I love you" to my Dad.

Realising this, I then rambled some more. I said I hoped I had always shown that I loved him, in everything I did and the way I acted. I said that I had chickened out of saying it these past few months, but I wanted to say it now to confirm that I did love him.

My Dad had been incredibly patient listening to my ramblings, and when I finished he said:

"You should still say it David."

"I know," I spoke softly. I was crying, and I can't remember at what point I had started crying.

"David reach into the drawer," I looked up expectantly. I recognised the significance of this moment. I made my final disclosure. Dad also apparently had one to make. I opened the drawer of his bedside table.

"Take my wallet."

I did.

"Inside there are two cards. Bank of Scotland and Clydesdale."

"Yeah Dad."

Dad then proceeded to tell me the details for his bank accounts! I had opened my soul and faced an existential crisis trying to work out what to tell Dad. Dad, pragmatic parent to the end, wanted to sort out the money!

I recorded these details on my phone, the note was saved at 16:32.

"I've done that Dad." I told him.

We sat there, father and son, our last rites to each other complete. I wasn't too sure how to fill the silence.

"I'm tired now David," Dad told me.

"Okay, I'll leave you to it." I got up and went to join the others.

Those were the last words my Dad ever said to me.

There was a small conservatory adjoined to Dad's room, a purpose-built family area for situations such as these. There was a glass door so that we could all still see Dad. As I entered someone asked me if I was okay. I gave a brave "Yeah".

"Would you like a cup of tea?" my niece asked me.

"Yes please." I gladly accepted the British solution to every problem.

One of my cousins swapped with me to be in the room with Dad, whilst the rest of the family told me a little more about the day. Dad had refused to take painkillers, wanting to be fully awake and alert for when I arrived. He had kept on looking at the clock throughout the day, and the rest of the family had been keeping him updated on my movements, telling him I would be there at about 4pm. Dad had held on for me through the day, and had finally taken painkillers just before I had arrived.

My aunt talked the most as I remember, telling us about Dad's childhood and she had some photos to show us. She was keeping the spirits up in the room.

The door opened, and my cousin poked her head in.

"His breathing's slowing down."

A hush fell on the room, and we moved through to congregate round Dad's bed. Dad seemed like he was in a trance, his eyes were half-closed and his breathing shallow. I returned once again to the side of his bed and held his hand. I kissed him on his big baldy head and said "Goodbye Dad."

My Dad had always said that when he was ready to die, he was going to go out into nature and enter a meditative state until his spirit passed over. In the end that was almost exactly what happened.

Dad had told the doctors that when the pain became too great, he wanted to be put to sleep. The painkillers that he had taken just before I arrived allowed him to do so. By the time we had gathered in his room, I'm not sure he had any sensory perception; perhaps hearing, which they say is the last thing to go.

It was a surreal experience sitting there and watching someone die. We all cried in fits and spurts, sometimes feeling a calmness in the situation, sometimes incredible pain at the approaching loss. I continued to hold Dad's hand throughout as I went through my waves of serenity and suffering. I remember I just kept on saying "Be at peace Dad", "Let go", "Be at peace".

Dad had one final game he wanted to play with us. One final tease. His breaths were coming in single spurts, the gaps between them lengthening. I swear at least three times we thought Dad had taken his final breath, so long was the gap between them. At one point we thought he was gone, and maybe thirty seconds later he let out a huge rasping breath that caused us all to jump! I think that one was his second last, because I made a point of remembering his last.

It's often described in books and Hollywood as a "death rattle", and I guess that isn't far from the truth. For me, bizarrely, it made me think of the beginning of *Citizen Kane* when he famously murmurs "Rosebud". When you're in those kind of situations, the mind seems to think of the craziest things. Maybe it was just because I wanted Dad's final breath to have some significance, or maybe Orson Welles actually did a very good interpretation of the "death rattle". Either way, after that last breath, there was a long silence. We figured that was him gone, and someone fetched a nurse. Dad was confirmed dead at just past 5pm.

The events following that confirmation were a bit haphazard. We talked, we hugged, we cried. One-by-one, the family started to leave to find space for their grief. I called my Dad's best friend to help me sort out the undertaker; I called my Mum to tell her the news, and I also called one of my close friends.

Soon it was just me and my girlfriend, sat in that conservatory. It had started raining profusely, so after I had made all those calls, I also called a taxi. I remember saying to my girlfriend more than once. "I just need to get out of here." "I want out of here".

Eventually I couldn't stand being in that space anymore, and I decided to wait at the front door for the taxi instead.

As we walked back through Dad's room, I looked back at him. His head had dropped onto one shoulder. His chin and jowls were bunched up, his mouth was open, and the corners were upturned.

"It looks like he's smiling, doesn't it?" I turned to my girlfriend with a small smile of my own.

"Yeah," she agreed.

I looked back at my Dad. I will always remember him as smiling. In death as he was in life. I stepped back though the curtain.

That was the last time I ever saw my Dad.

And this is the first time I have ever fully disclosed what happened during the last 60 minutes of Dad's life.

Introduction

I'll return to speaking about Dad a little later, but first I'd like to clarify why I'm writing this book. You see, I think too many of us are taking our lives for granted; I know I certainly was. The many people who are not taking care of their diet are taking their lives for granted. The people staying in unfulfilling jobs are taking their lives for granted. The people putting off their dreams until some vague "tomorrow" are taking their lives for granted. I have seen that in one breath we can be here, and in the next we are gone.

I see far too many people that do not realise how important their lives are, or what the important things in their lives really are. There is too much pursuit of material worth, and not enough for priceless experiences. There is too much lazy acceptance of current conditions, and not enough striving for self-growth and mastery. There are too many people living in a narrow view of the world, and not enough expansion into new and wonderful perspectives. There is too much hate, anger and jealously, and not enough acceptance, co-operation and love. There are too many people catering to ego-centric needs, and not enough people seeking to impact and contribute to the world. There is nothing like death to give you a perspective on life. I see the world through such a different lens now. I see what we really need to do to live a fulfilled life.

Because too many people are living an unfulfilled life. I see people living in poor health. I see people suffering from a range of emotional disorders. I see people hating their jobs. I see people putting up with toxic relationships. To see all this suffering makes me sad. It is almost worst than death. Because if we are not living our lives to their fullest potential, then why are we even here?

Nevertheless, I detect a change. We are in an exciting new age of innovation and connection. There is a shift in health and wellbeing. We are no longer blind to the implications of the types of food we are putting in our body or the consequences of a lack of activity. Our construction of relationships has become more diverse. Sexual expression is far more open, the LGBT community have become increasingly accepted and recognised, the "nuclear family" construction of heterosexuality is interpreted and practiced in more diverse ways. Finally, I do sense an intellectual and spiritual "awakening"; a desire to find purpose and meaning in the world. Yoga and meditation has soared in popularity; an exciting generation of entrepreneurs passionate about contribution has emerged; and more people are attending self-development events and reading self-help books (case study #1 is you right now!).

In our exciting new world, there are of course a new set of challenges. The internet and media have exacerbated the pressure on creating a public identity for oneself. It is difficult to live authentically in a very judgemental world. The instant gratification nature of click-and-receive has led to a sense of entitlement. Society has laid out a script for how we're supposed to live, and when this doesn't work out for us we get frustrated and angry. Consequently, these ramped-up stresses and pressures have made us more susceptible to negative emotions and mood disorders. It is hard to find and commit to the time to work on yourself. There is also conflict in relationships at the micro-level (divorce, infidelity, sexism, homophobia) and at the macro-level (war, racism, xenophobia).

Nonetheless, I am optimistic that all these challenges can be worked on and overcome, and that is what ignited my desire to write this book. I want to lift people's spirits and show them how to live with joy and abundance. I want them to rediscover themselves and align with their purpose and life's mission. I want every person to be able to form deep and meaningful relationships and create a world of harmony and co-operation. It took the loss of someone I loved to create this passion in me, and to start to work towards these things in my life. I don't want you to go through that same pain. I don't want you to have to go through some horrific life event before you generate the impetus to change. I hope that through hearing an account of my pain, you will not have to go through the pain yourself.

In this book you are going to find a reason for living again. Each of you reading this has had a set of hardships and challenges. Things you have struggled with and perhaps are still struggling with. What I want to tell you is that these experiences are gifts. They might not feel like it but they have shaped you, given you strength and perspective, taught you lessons that could not have been acquired in any other way.

I understand and connect with your pain, because I've been through a lot of pain too. Not just Dad's death. I have had a series of hardships throughout my life, culminating in the greatest hardship which was of course losing Dad.

But you see the thing is, losing my dad was simultaneously the worst and greatest thing that ever happened to me. I experienced pain on a level I had never felt before, but I also gained perspective that I would've never found otherwise. It ignited a drive and passion in me that I never had before. It reconnected me with parts of myself that had long been hidden away, a lot of inner power. I would not be here writing this book, seeking to influence the world, if Dad had not passed. From all my hardships I have learned to see the gift in them. I recognise that each of these things needed to happen exactly the way they did to get me to where I am today. By the end of this book, I hope you will also see your life in the same way.

Dad's death was a final piece in the puzzle and what I needed to put me on my current path. Since his death I have come to understand the path to living a fulfilled life, and that is what I'm going to share with you in this book. This book will help you connect with what's really important in life, and help you walk the path to a higher form of living.

Now before we move on, I want to stimulate your mind with some questions. As I will reveal later, one of the key components of this new life for yourself is reflection and acting on insight. At the end of each chapter I am going to have some activities that I would highly recommend you engage in. You can of course skip over these and keep reading; you can give them a half-hearted response. Both are fine, but you will get out of this book whatever you put into it.

I want to make a pact with you. I have invested a lot into this book. When I wrote that last chapter, tears were pouring down my face. I connected with that pain again so that I could give you the full value of my experience. I have outlined my deepest insights and most effective strategies in this book. Will you meet me halfway and fully awaken your own transformation? Will you dedicate yourself to change and growth? Will you take your life in an exciting new direction? If you agree to this pact, then you agree to give these questions some time. They don't take hours or days, and you will earn back this time tenfold by shortening your growth curve. If you're willing, grab yourself a pen and paper, and let's do this:

Questions and Activities

Complete these sentences.

1. What is holding me back most in life right now is...

2. If you're honest with yourself, the things that you are putting up with just now are...

3. I can take more care of myself by...

4. I am motivated to change because...

Chapter 1: Dad and Me

In the previous chapter I outlined the challenges I see in the world currently. I theorised on the hardships you may have suffered and the reasons why you may be reading this book. The way I see the world and the empathy I have with your struggles was not bestowed on me at birth. I am not some omniscient and benevolent demigod, graced with the understanding of life, the universe, and everything by purely existing. I had to learn a lot of hard lessons. Life punched me in the eye several times until I was able to really see and understand the world around me. The universe has placed challenge after challenge in my path to teach, develop and sculpt me into the person I am today.

My education started at four years old, when Dad and Mum got divorced. This was a painful experience for me, and I will elaborate further on this later. However, the crux of the matter was that my first experience of love and connection was sullied, and it left me with a lot of unresolved attachment and emotional issues that I then carried into later life.

Nonetheless, full credit to my parents, they both invested so much in me. My Dad was always stimulating my philosophical and spiritual mind. We took frequent walks in nature, and he would ask me questions on the "energy" I felt, what I thought about life and death, talking about the power of the mind. We would listen to tapes by Wayne Dyer and Deepak Chopra everywhere we went. Mum was always cultivating my creativity and imagination: playing with Lego, baking, visiting science centres. She would draw and do puzzles with me, take part in my role playing games, read to me before bed each night.

Yet still I had a number of underlying problems: internalising my emotions, struggling to integrate with others, an inability to deal with challenging situations. When I moved up to secondary school, this all hit me in a big way. I was unhappy emotionally and socially. I didn't like who I was, and I didn't fit in to the new environment. I was subject to bullying and disrespect from my peers.

So I developed two coping mechanisms. The first was binge eating. I would stuff myself with food, and poor food at that. One particular vice was crisps, and I once ate an entire 20-pack in one day. So my weight ballooned and by the time I was 13 I weighed 17 stone. I was left with stretch marks on my belly which I still have to this day.

The second was that I switched to an alter-ego. I saw that my current identity, my authentic identity, was not accepted. So I put on a mask; betraying my authentic self, and becoming the model they wanted me to be. I became the class clown, acting out, not bothering to do my work, getting put in detention. I changed the way I spoke and the words that I used. Again, at age 13, this approach culminated in a low point, getting suspended from school for three days for "happy slapping" another pupil (does anyone remember that trend? YouTube it. I'm not proud of it.).

At age 13 I had reached a real trough in my life. I was sickened by what I had let myself become. I hated how I looked. My self-esteem and confidence were down the pan. But I had now reached the moment of Critical Mass. I define the moment of Critical Mass as the moment when you become more scared of staying the same than you are of changing. I now wanted to do something about the situation, and luckily my Dad was there to help me.

As soon as I had developed those stretch marks. I had hid changing in front of people, at school and at home. One day, however, my guard slipped and Dad saw the marks. This was about the time that I had decided to make my change, and seeing how my habits and emotions had disfigured me so tangibly, Dad resolved to help me.

Together Dad and I embarked on an increased awareness of activity and healthy eating. I started to play sports and monitor my diet. It was a tough couple of years. I struggled constantly with my image and self-esteem, as well as in my relationships. I was a damaged and vulnerable push-over, making me the subject of bullying and teasing. As a defence mechanism, I still had the persona of class-clown and "rebel", but this alienated people who might otherwise have been my friends. I was confused about who I was trying and wanted to be.

Eventually by age 16 I had dropped down to a much healthier 13 stone. I was playing in three sports teams and going to the gym. My confidence and self-esteem were still shaky, but by then I had found an effective bandage for that: alcohol. I still struggled in forming relationships, especially with the opposite sex, but reading some books on how to pick up women helped there (again especially when alcohol was involved!). It was at this age myself and my peers were also starting to plan our future careers, and here Dad made an incisive contribution.

He had been a fantastic support over those three years, coming to watch me at sports games, spending hours each week helping me practice, allowing me to have parties so that I could foster and strengthen my relationships. But one small suggestion of his proved to be the most significant.

At 16 we had a school careers evening. Practitioners from loads of different fields came in and we were given short slots to interview them. We were allocated three interviews and I could only think of two I wanted to speak to: a journalist, and a historian. I told Dad I didn't know what to do for my third choice so I showed him the sheet of people coming in.

"There's a psychologist here," my Dad said. "I think psychology would suit you. Why don't you speak to her?"

I didn't have a better suggestion, so I agreed. Of course the careers evening came around, and the journalist and historian managed to put me off pursuing their careers, and the psychologist inspired me. I knew what I wanted to do when I left school.

By now I had finally found a bit of direction in life. I had managed to build up an identity for myself that got me more respect. I had a group of friends. I had a vision for the future. However, the identity I had built was not an authentic one. I had good relationships, but I always guarded myself in them, giving less than the other person in every interaction. I was on the right path for my future, but I hadn't quite found my inner song.

The biggest problem was that I had changed my external circumstances, but not my internal reality. I still saw myself as the fat kid, even though I wasn't anymore. I was still terrified of social rejection, even though I hide behind a wall of bravado. I was interested in my new career, but I hadn't yet tapped into my passion.

An incident happened when I was 17 that brought back all my insecurities with a sickening crunch. I was dating someone, and another guy was jealous of us. One night my girlfriend and I were walking home, and he recruited four of his friends to beat me up in front of her. I have never been so helpless and humiliated, and it hit upon all my unresolved issues, all the feelings of inadequacy I had hidden away. To add insult to injury, she left me about a month later for another guy, and rightly or wrongly I linked that with those feelings of helplessness and inadequacy.

These events snapped something in me, and put me into a very dangerous pattern of thinking. That if I had looked different, that if I had been leaner and more muscular, those guys would never have touched me. If I had been leaner and more muscular, my girlfriend would never have left me. So I started to exercise excessively. I went from going to the gym 3 times a week to 6. Each workout lasting about an hour and a half. I then went away to university and stopped playing all the sports I had loved to dedicate myself to the gym. When the changes that I desired weren't happening, I notched on an hour of swimming after those hour and a half workouts.

I became more and more neurotic about what I ate, how much I ate, and when I ate. I stuck to the same "safe" foods. I restricted portion sizes and stuck to low-fat, low calorie foods. I ate at 9am, noon, 3pm, 6pm and 9pm on the dot because I read somewhere that was the best way to build muscle and lose weight. I remember being home during the holidays and Dad made meatballs and spaghetti for dinner, with seven meatballs. I threw one in the bin because I only "allowed" myself six.

Then in my second year of university, I started to self-medicate and seek happiness through alcohol, partying and sex. I was drinking 4, 5, even 6 nights a week, and heavy drinking at that. I would think nothing of polishing off half a bottle of rum while watching a film.

Of course with alcohol comes calories, so I continued to try and do my excessive workouts. As I was often hungover and fatigued, I started drinking coffee like it was going out of fashion and popping caffeine pills like skittles. I resorted to more and more extreme methods to restrict my food intake and calories. Instead of meals I was chewing sticks of gum until my stomach stopped rumbling. Counting a tablespoon of cottage cheese as a "meal".

Eventually my body could no longer handle this abuse, and three months into my second year of university it collapsed on me. I developed a horrendous full-body rash, and started suffering from insomnia. I was too tired and ill to exercise and couldn't sustain the willpower and motivation to restrict myself as fiercely as I had been. I was helpless and vulnerable, ready to be ensnared by a new demon: depression.

2012 was the worst year of my life. For that calendar year Depression floored me. I was tired all the time, but couldn't sleep. I was struggling through basic everyday tasks, trying to stay on track at university. All the things that used to bring me joy - music, films, friends, exploring - brought me nothing. I was living in an empty, emotionless void. I was waking up in the morning and wondering where I could find the energy to trudge through another sapping, unfulfilling day. Then there were some mornings when I wished I hadn't woken up at all.

I felt so lost and lonely. I eventually confided in Dad, and only because he asked me directly if I was feeling depressed. I'll never forget the piece of advice he gave me: "Try to find and focus on the small victories each day." That is advice that I have continued to follow, in good times as well as bad, and it is the advice I give to others when they are struggling.

On New Year's Day 2013, I had again reached a moment of critical mass. I was no longer prepared to keep on putting up with the state my life was in. I wanted something better for myself, and I was determined to work out how to achieve that.

Towards the end of 2012, I had decided to reignite a lifelong dream. From as early as I can remember, I had always wanted to be an author. I always had my head in books and constantly role-played fantasy worlds. From the age of 5 or 6, when teachers asked us what we wanted to be when we grew up, I had always said "author". But I quickly learnt that wasn't "cool" and it wasn't a dream that my teachers particularly encouraged, so I put it off for *fifteen* years. In my darkest moments I returned to it, and I started to find solace in escaping to another world with my writing. I made my pact at the start of 2013 that I was going to make this dream become a reality.

In May 2013, I published my first book, and in August 2014 my second. My Dad was proofreader and editor for both. I started to empower myself through exercise, using it to challenge me and teach me lessons about growth, rather than as a way to cure my feelings of inadequacy. I pushed myself in leadership roles, becoming Vice President and then President of the University Psychology Society. I studied hard and worked on my mindset to rediscover joy again in life, and to overcome my negative thought patterns.

In my final year of university I recognised I could use the lessons learned from my struggles, combined with my knowledge and passion for psychology and personal development, to help others overcome their challenges and hardships. I decided that once university finished I was going to start a business helping people create a better life for themselves.

I phoned Dad in November 2014 to tell him I had made this realisation. All of his teaching, those Wayne Dyer tapes, pointing me towards psychology, supporting me with my depression and writing, had come to fruition. I had found my path. He said he could hear the passion and energy in my voice, and that this really pleased him. He said he would help me by pointing me to useful articles and books.

A month later, on Christmas Eve, Dad went into hospital for a scan after a minor heart attack. But the problem was not in his heart. It was in his lungs and liver. Huge cancerous growths. Based on the spread and severity of the tumours, the doctors told him he had only 6-8 months to live.

Dad made the decision not to tell me for the final semester of university, so I could finish my studies without distraction. He visited at Easter and I saw he had lost a lot of weight. He told me he was off the booze and eating healthy. I bought it and praised him on a job well done.

Well he told me the truth on May 27th. I'll always remember the moment. I had just come back to my flat after an early morning appointment. My bedroom door was directly opposite the front door, and one of my flatmates had left an envelope outside my door. I looked down and recognised Dad's handwriting. *'Probably a congratulations card'* I thought.

It was a letter. Dad, in old-fashioned, awkward male fashion, broke the news to me in this letter. At that point he was approaching the six month mark after his diagnosis. I called him to ask him more about it. He explained the situation very matter-of-factly. He said he was largely comfortable and in little pain. He even asked if I had a cold! I said "No Dad, I'm crying". I had to laugh about how nonchalant Dad was about the situation, when I felt my world had shattered.

That day my friend and I were running focus groups for the business, and I walked round to his place with tears running down my face. The focus groups helped me take my mind off it for the day, but in the evening it all hit me again and I bawled my eyes out. I tried to get on with life in the next couple of days, but I ended up having to run home from the gym or the shops as the tears flooded out.

After the initial shock, I realised that I needed to make the most of whatever time we had left. I visited Dad the following week and interviewed him about his life. This was partly for my benefit, so I had no unanswered questions; partly for the benefit of others, as I asked Dad for his lessons and perspective that he had picked up from a life filled with tough hardships and fascinating experiences. It was a magical three hour experience where I learnt and understood so much about my Dad, and I will treasure that memory for the rest of my life. I have that record of Dad's voice and teaching whenever I need guidance or comfort.

I gave Dad a gratitude letter, outlining everything I was grateful to him for over the years. When I left him at the train station, he offered the usual manly handshake we shared together. I instead hugged him. What I really wanted to do was also tell him that I loved him. But I bottled it. I guess I knew that admission meant that I was losing him, and I was still struggling to face that reality.

I saw him another weekend, and then my eyes were on my approaching graduation. It was something I had been anticipating for a couple of years. It was an important personal achievement obviously, but what it really offered me was a unique opportunity. My graduation was going to bring my parents together for the first time in eighteen years. For just a single day, it would feel like I had a normal family life. The life I have craved and lacked for as long as I could remember. It had already been a once-in-a-lifetime opportunity, and Dad's diagnosis had really emphasised that fact.

The day before my graduation, my Dad called me. In the last week he had developed Jaundice. The cancer was affecting his liver's ability to process toxins. He was suffering from cramps, had liquid coming out of both ends, and was feeling fatigued.

"I'm really sorry son, I'm not going to be able to make your graduation."

I felt like he had told me about his diagnosis all over again. My dad was tough in body and mind, and he would have pushed through a lot of pain and discomfort to get to my graduation. But it was a three-hour journey, and if Dad said he couldn't make it, I knew he couldn't make it. I had looked forward to this moment for so long. After finding out about Dad's cancer, I had especially looked towards this day as a moment of closure, a final happy memory I could have of my Dad.

But I never got it. I made the best of it on the day, and I did have a good time with just my mum and gran. However, I would've swapped a few of the short years Dad and I spent together, or even a few of my own, to have had him there that day. You can have all the ceremony and success in the world, but without love, it feels hollow. I could've been crowned the best student in the history of the university, but without my Dad there it wouldn't have meant that much.

I made up for it somewhat by visiting him the next weekend. My friend and I went up to visit to show him pictures and videos from the graduation. Dad was in good spirits, but he was looking really unwell by this point.

You know the story from here. As the jaundice set in, Dad deteriorated and was taken into hospital. My girlfriend and I visited him there, and as we got the bus home, I cried on my girlfriend's shoulder, wondering if that would be the last time I ever saw my dad.

The following Tuesday, 21st of July, was actually Dad's birthday! I called him and asked how he was doing, joking that it probably didn't rank as one of his better birthdays. Dad was upbeat and sounded strong. He said he was on some new medication that was easing his pain and fatigue. He told me his operation was scheduled for Thursday. I thought to myself that if this was successful, and they were able to drain some of the toxins from him, he might have weeks left.

Of course, that was not the case, and on the 24th I spent my final living moments with Dad. Ten days later, I delivered the eulogy at his funeral. A couple of weeks later I scattered his ashes at Eilean Donan Castle in Scotland, the ancestral stronghold of Clan Macrae.

And that is where this book begins. You see, unintentionally (although I suspect by very intentional universal design), I began writing this book, writing that prologue, exactly a year to the day from scattering Dad's ashes. Everything now contained in this book is what I have learned and realised since saying that final goodbye. Dad's death was an absolute game-changer for me, and I grew and matured more as a person in this last year than the previous five years I had spent at university. As I'm sure some of you have spotted from the dates I have given, I am far from some old wise guru. I write this approaching my 24th birthday, and the book as a whole will be released shortly after I turn 24.

I say this to inspire you as to how quickly change can occur in your life and how rapidly you can create something better for yourself. If a young man in the depths of grief can create a better life for himself, then you can too. Dad taught me many things, but there were a few things he could only teach me through his death. His death taught me the value of life. His death taught me what the important things in life are. His death has given me a drive and purpose to share my message. His death has helped me to live a life of love and service, and to spread that love and service to as many people as I can. This is what I hope to impart to you throughout the rest of this book.

Questions and Activities

1. Write about a time you lost something important. Try to see the "gift" in that loss. What did you gain/learn/develop from that loss?

2. Do you have a loss that still brings you pain? Keep a journal and document the moments when you feel this loss. One of the most helpful elements in my grieving process was externalising and processing my emotions through writing and I would encourage you to do the same.

3. How can you create meaning from that loss? What action can you take or message can you spread to make that loss mean something?

4. Write down a list of all the things your parents have done for you, and how that has shaped who you are today (even the bad things. If you had a poor relationship with your parents, that has still developed the strengths and skills in you that you have today).

5. Ring your parents, and tell them how much you love them. I nearly missed the chance to tell my Dad I loved him. I would especially recommend this if you are estranged from your parent(s). It might just be the thing that brings you together.

Chapter 2: As It Stands

Let's look at the state of affairs just now, because if you're reading this book, I'm sure that you're of a similar mindset to me…things need to change, don't they? I identify three prominent issues in our society right now: emotional, intellectual, and spiritual. Three areas where huge barriers, faulty mindsets and incomplete education are impairing our growth. Levels of many categorised mental health disorders are on the rise. In particular, rates of anxiety and depression are soaring. Huge swathes of the population are stuck in unfulfilling careers and life paths, lacking direction and vibrancy for their futures. Our relationships are increasingly filled with tension and conflict, both at the interpersonal and international level.

Conversely, our world is also on the cusp of some very exciting change. We are progressing rapidly on multiple fronts such as technology, innovation and science. The internet has democratised information and connected the thought-leaders of the world to each other and to their students. Whilst we have many big challenges to confront, we have more people than ever working on their solutions.

Since embarking on my personal and professional journey I have been encouraged by the number of service-driven teachers I have come across, many of whom are providing incredibly valuable content for free. I also sense a shift in consciousness. People aren't content with their current circumstances, and they want to make a change. Nonetheless, I feel this awareness is shifting slowly, and there are still too many people in society sticking their heads in the sand and putting up with their pain. What I hope I can achieve with this book is to inspire people to confront their pain and overcome it.

Emotional Wellness

Let's examine these challenges in a little more detail, firstly looking at our emotional epidemic. Rates of anxiety and depression are shooting through the roof. People are burnt-out and stressed at work. They are apathetic and dull in their everyday interactions, and what are our current coping strategies? Medication and self-medication. For every major mental health disorder we have half a dozen drugs to combat it. There are also a lot of people who like to write themselves their own prescriptions: junk food, tobacco and alcohol often being the medication of choice, with some opting for the hard, illegal stuff.

All these substances are just covering up our problems. They are giving us a way to ignore, neglect and devalue our self-care and the importance of addressing our issues head-on. Walk through any city centre between 12am-3am on a Saturday and Sunday Morning and you will see a host of people covering up their problems rather than addressing them. Don't get me wrong; I'm not judging these individuals. I used to do the same myself. I've had my struggles with mental health. I used to drink like a fish because it was easier than working on myself and confronting my issues.

I see some progress to addressing this concern. The stigma around mental health problems is reducing. Wide-scale initiatives such as mindfulness are being rolled out and having success. Progressive employers have started to implement serious strategies to look after the wellbeing of their employees. However, I would like to see this on a wider scale, and to shift our mentality towards our emotional wellness from cure to prevention.

I think we have to learn how to practice "Emotional First Aid" as Guy Winch advocates in his book of this name. We need to understand and use strategies to address minor psychological wounds, before they become infected and chronic. We need to recognise the necessity to look after our emotional health in the same way as our physical health: with good habits and consistent practice.

I believe the default setting of our society needs to be shifted. Our news is negative. Our television is negative. Our social media creates a mindset of constant comparison. Our workplaces are high stress environments. We love to moan and complain. We love drama. We give more airtime and attention to Donald Trump, The Kardashians, and Katie Hopkins than Adam Braun, Brendon Burchard, and Elon Musk (I suspect some of you reading this have no idea who they are do you? Look them up and see what they're doing for the world. Consider if perhaps they are worth a bit more airtime than who we currently focus on). If we shift our default setting to "positive", then perhaps people will have less things to be depressed and anxious about.

Intellectual Purpose

I'm saddened to see many people wandering through life without conscious design. They have settled into a life that was chosen for them, or gotten comfortable with a mediocre one. Too many people are going to look back from their deathbed and wonder where all those years of their life went. I'm sure some of you reading this resonate with my earlier story. Of how I used to wake up in the morning and wonder why the hell I was even bothering to get out of bed. Employment is one of our biggest sources of emotional turmoil, and here I see a huge source of dissatisfaction in our society. You see society has sold us a script on how to find success and happiness. It goes something like this:

1. Work hard in school. Get good grades. Go to higher education.
2. Work hard in higher education. Get good grades. Get yourself a degree/qualification
3. Use this degree/qualification to get yourself a well-paying job. Devote 5/7 of your life to this job.
4. Use the money from this job for occasional holidays, buying furniture, cars and houses.
5. Meet, live with, and marry a member of the opposite sex. Have children.
6. Retire in the eighth decade of your life with a pension. Use this pension for all the things you're now too old to do.
7. Support your children to jump on the same conveyor belt you just jumped off of.

Now I'm not saying that this model doesn't work for everyone. I'm not saying some people aren't incredibly fulfilled with their jobs. I'm not saying some people don't have an incredible and loving family. I'm not saying some people look back on their life path with nothing but fondness. I'm not even saying there is anything inherently wrong with this model. The first problem is that this is not a path that suits everyone. The second problem with any framework is that without education on how to implement it, your chances of success with it are very low.

Let's demonstrate this by outlining one of my favourite frameworks: Stephen Covey's *7 Habits of Highly Effective People.*

1. Be Proactive
2. Begin with the End in Mind
3. Put First Things First
4. Think Win-Win
5. Seek First to Understand, then to be Understood
6. Synergise
7. Sharpen the Saw

For those of you who have read Stephen's book, you'll appreciate how incredibly valuable this framework can be for transforming your life. For those of you who haven't, you have no idea how to navigate this framework do you? That's because you haven't been educated on how to use this framework, how to implement it in your life, and how to use it to enhance your happiness and success. Guess which framework we're not educated on either? That framework I outlined above that society tells us *to live our life by.*

Well there is some change filtering in at various stages of the framework. Progressive companies such as Google and Apple are throwing out the script on dictating to their employees how to work and instead empowering their employees to work on their own projects that provide them with meaning and purpose. I embarked on the entrepreneurial journey because I didn't like the script society has presented us, and I have seen a surge of others doing the same.

Universities are instigating programs to provide clarity to their students on how they want the script of the rest of their lives to read. In my third year of university we did a module called Professional Skills that flipped the switch on my life, it gave me so much clarity on my mission and direction for the future. Nonetheless, I still graduated with far too many intelligent, talented and hard-working individuals *who didn't have a clue* about what they wanted from their lives. If we can't give people clarity and direction in a decade and a half of constant education, then the way I see it there is something seriously wrong with the system.

I think the solution lies in creating new educational initiatives from the ground up. I'm not talking about the superficial rebranding that happens every few years. I'm talking about an absolute paradigm shift. Encourage children to build their character virtues rather than their academic and professional virtues. Bring visualisation activities, goal-setting and meditation into the curriculum. Make it fun so that these things don't just become habits, they become necessities.

Don't test knowledge and memory the way we currently do, test creativity and the application of knowledge: replace multiple choice with role play; ask the students to give presentations on their favourite parts of a topic, rather than write essays on parts they didn't enjoy. I don't know about you, but anything I didn't like went out of my head as soon as I finished the test or exam on it. Conversely, I still remember writing or talking about the things I was passionate about.

For the adults who have missed this opportunity, I think we need to make Personal Development trendy, attainable, and relevant.

- **Trendy:** It is a badge of honour to say you have completed a marathon, seen your favourite artist live and watched the latest Netflix phenomenon. Let's make it trendy to have completed a meditation retreat, seen your favourite thought leader live and done your journaling.

- **Attainable:** The field has some fantastic role models - Tony Robbins, Tim Ferriss, Oprah Winfrey - but the magnitude of their achievements and the dedication to their growth can be daunting. Instead of trying to emulate Tony's phenomenal mindset shifts, Tim's liberating time and productivity frameworks, and Oprah's powerful communication skills, let's have "gateway" projects. Apps on our phone with exercises that we can draw upon whenever we feel negative thoughts; 30-day challenge forums where the members keep each other motivated and accountable; more international groups society where people can come together to share their lessons and insights on growth.

- **Relevant:** Finally people often don't do Personal Development because it generally doesn't have any obvious and immediate incentive. Our inner work is often a long, abstract process. Let's make this stuff matter on CVs and applications. Projects like the Duke of Edinburgh Award stand out on university applications, let's have more projects which carry a similar weight. A first aid qualification can be a nice add-on for a CV, how about also having an *emotional* first aid qualification. If there's one thing that creates relevancy, it's money. Let's have projects and programs whereby employers will pay you a higher salary. That will get people interested!

<u>Spiritual Connection</u>

I think my biggest concern in our world right now is relationships. The world has opened up to people of different colours, cultures and creeds. We are now intermingled in a way like never before, yet this has given birth to the ugliness of racism, xenophobia, homophobia and religious war. Advances certainly have been made, and I'm encouraged by the progress, but I write this in 2016, the year of Brexit and Donald Trump. The year of religious terrorism and racist shootings. A climate of fear and intolerance has been bred. There is conflict between Christian and Muslim, White and Black, Conservative and Liberal. I think we have taken some scary backward steps in how we relate to our fellow human being.

I also see problems at the micro-level of relationships. Divorce rates are at 50%. A study was done in the UK recently and it found that 19% of people in a relationship are either about to break it up,or are seriously considering it. *This is crazy*. What has made us lose connection with each other?

I think social media has ironically made us less social. Now likes and instant messaging constitute communication. I sometimes sit in a coffee shop or restaurant and I'll see boyfriend and girlfriend sitting opposite each other scrolling on their phones. I sometimes see groups of FOUR or even MORE people all sitting scrolling. If you can't find something to talk about between four of you, there is something seriously wrong with your willingness or ability to communicate.

Once more, I hold my hands up and say I've been there and done it. I used to be obsessed with the image I was projecting out into the world, in real life and of course on the internet. I had everything on my phone: Facebook, Instagram, Snapchat, Tinder, anything to gain me social gratification. I struggled to form intimate relationships with people for a long time, particularly romantically. I had a lot of unresolved attachment issues and low feelings of self-worth, and I apologise to all my ex-girlfriends for failing to give them the attention and emotional commitment they deserved. I think there are a lot of people in the same situation as I was, and it's killing our relationships.

I do see some promising changes. Scandinavia is leading the way in introducing paternity leave, a recognition of the importance of full family support and engagement. Childcare is not the mother's duty, it is a venture to be undertaken by both parents. More balance (and thus less tension) can be created in the relationship and family. Huge strides have been made in introducing gay marriage, particularly in the U.S. in 2015. The internet is also being used to bring people together in more meaningful ways, through websites such as meetup.com. Organisations such as Toastmasters are striving to make people better communicators.

Nonetheless, I see huge room for improvement. If we cannot get off our phones for half an hour to engage with a friend, how are we ever going to overcome difficulties in our marriages? If the only thing we strive for is the superficial value of likes and internet friends how are we ever going to understand the spiritual perspective of people from other religions? If we can't get out of the insular worlds of seeking to validate our own identities, how will we ever be able to understand and accept the identities of people from a different country; who have a different sexuality; or even just a different political perspective?

I think we need to create social "phone fines", severe penalties for choosing cyber communication over real communication. I know some people instruct everyone to stack their phone in the middle of the table at dinner, and whoever picks their phone up first also picks up the bill. I think we also need to have the self-discipline to remove ourselves from our phones. Whenever I have an important engagement (personally or professionally) my phone goes onto airplane mode, because on silent you will still get distracted by the vibrations.

I also believe that social interaction is something that we should put on our timetables and schedules. We need to treat social interactions with the same urgency and respect as appointments and meetings. We also need to create quality time. Going to the cinema with a friend is not quality time. Sitting in a coffee shop scrolling through Instagram is not quality time. Sitting in a bar watching the game is not quality time. Many of us are sharing time with each other, not spending time with each other.

Now I'm not telling you to not go to the cinema, share videos and pictures or watch sports, but this cannot be your only form of communication. Couples are spending their evenings glued to their phones or televisions (or both!) and wondering why they are having communication problems. The average person spends four hours a day in front of a screen, I think we can all reallocate that time more wisely.

Finally, we require projects that allow us to integrate with people of different cultures and different worldviews. In our new globalised world, travel and communication has been made easier than ever. Travel is something that is practiced well in the young and middle-class, with gap years and study abroad schemes. As a result students are the most inclusive and accepting group of people I have ever spent time with.

At my university I was proud to have friends who were Black, German, Bisexual, Muslim and Working-class. You see I learnt far more from these friends then I did from the White, English-speaking, Heterosexual, Christian, Middle-class friends that I spent most of my time growing up with. However, I find this inclusion and tolerance decreases outside the student population, and I think the two obvious factors for this are travel and education.

I propose that we have schemes for travel and education built into our schooling system (it always comes back to school doesn't it? These things need to be foundational). I think we need more exchange schemes built into the curriculum. These would not be mandatory, as that is draconian and not suited to everyone, but they should be positively incentivised by carrying weight in interviews and applications. Even if students chose not to go abroad, they would have the benefit of having people from other countries and cultures come to them.

I recognise that we do have such schemes, but I believe they are poorly structured and don't actively try to promote integration and connection. Similar programs should be available after leaving education, or for those who don't go to university where such programs are well established. In the U.K. we used to have mandatory national service, but wouldn't it be a thing to have mandatory *international service*?

Instead of serving our country for the purposes of war and conflict, how about we serve other countries for the purposes of peace and co-operation? There are a number of great voluntary schemes active, but because they are voluntary, only the people from privileged backgrounds can afford to undertake them. Let's give people a wage for the work that they do. Then after seeing the conditions of countries such as Somalia and Palestine, they might understand some of the violence and religious hate that is fostered and bred in such countries. We cannot solve a problem unless we have an understanding of it.

<u>The Progressive Society</u>

The people who are going to thrive in our new world will be those who are able to look past and overcome negativity and struggle. They will be equipped with tools and mindsets that allow them to recognise that negativity is both inevitable and temporary, and how to process and move past it. They will be people who take a conscious decision to work on themselves and their purpose. They will understand the nature of incremental process, and the importance of living a life aligned with their values. Such individuals will also possess the skills and focus to foster deep and meaningful connections with others. They will seek to create communities based on co-operation and creation.

Everything that I have outlined to you in this chapter came to me in a very short period of time. Dad's looming death stimulated a lot of thinking about life, and I started to see the world in a very different light. The key junction, however, came during those last sixty minutes. Do you remember those three things I said to Dad? It took the imminency of death to collect my thoughts, but sometimes we need that critical stimulus to bring us clarity.

In that moment when I realised this would be the last time I spoke to Dad, I said three things:

"Thank you for the fantastic job you did of raising me; I'm incredibly proud to be your son; I love you Dad."

Unwittingly, I had stumbled upon the three solutions to the challenges I raised above. Three things that all of us should cultivate in our lives. These things must be important, otherwise I wouldn't have felt the urge to say them during our last conversation. From what I said, you can identify three components.

1. Gratitude
2. Identity
3. Love

Three solutions to three crises. We can mend our emotional wellness through expressing gratitude. We can find our intellectual purpose through cultivating our identity. We can repair our spiritual connection through giving love. Over the next three chapters, I am going to outline how to create a life based around these principles, and point you towards the phenomenal change they can create.

Questions and Activities

1. A negative emotion I am experiencing strongly right now is...

2. Identify a negative behaviour or context that is exacerbating this emotion. How can you remove this source of negativity from your life? What positive influence can you bring into your life to counteract this negative emotion?

3. Given the choice, the calling I really want to pursue in life is...

4. What steps can you take to advancing towards this calling? What practices can you do that are trendy, attainable and relevant to your current lifestyle?

5. The area of relationships where I need to work harder is...

6. How can I reallocate my time to give more priority to my relationships?

Chapter 3: Gratitude

"Thank you for the fantastic job you did of raising me"

The dream faded. My alarm blared angrily, and in a couple of seconds my reality sunk back in. I had returned to the emptiness of my waking life. I wished I could cut the cord that was keeping me in this reality, and I could return to live in the world of my dream.

It was the summer of 2012, and I was working on a children's camp in America. I had been suffering from depression for six months, and I had hoped that this trip would bring some life back for me, but all it had done was weaken my fragile relationship with it.

I had struggled to make friends. My misery had made me poor company, and the rest of my lifeguard team didn't really talk to me, with the exception of one, who sadly worked on the other side of the lake. I was missing my friends back home, who were all posting photos showing the fun they were having without me.

I was still in the grips of my eating disorder, and I hated the way I looked. Every day I had to go on the dock in just a pair of shorts and expose my disgusting body to everyone at camp. I was tired every day because I wasn't eating enough food to give me energy.

I was teaching children how to swim, and some of them were making amazing progress, but their achievements brought me no satisfaction.

It was gorgeous sunshine nearly every day. I was working on a camp with a lake, woods, hills. I was in a new country meeting new people. Yet I had no appreciation for the environment I was in.

Despite my worst efforts, I had actually attracted the attention of not one, but two girls, who were always trying to spend time with me. I disregarded their warmth. I was pining over not one, not two, but three ex-flames I had left behind in the UK.

I was ungrateful for their compassion; I was ungrateful for my beautiful surroundings; I was ungrateful for the opportunity for exploration and adventure; I was ungrateful for the contribution I was making to the lives of some of the poorest children in New York; I was ungrateful for the wonderful instrument the human body is; I was ungrateful for the connection I had with my fellow lifeguard Greg; *I was even ungrateful to be alive.*

It is no coincidence that the unhappiest period of my life was characterised by my lowest level of gratitude. You see gratitude is the second most powerful emotion we can experience, behind love. Gratitude allows us to rise above negativity. Gratitude allows us to overcome hardship. Gratitude allows us to enhance the positivity in our lives. Losing my Dad was the most painful experience in my life, but it was not the unhappiest, because I was constantly expressing gratitude in the lead up to his death.

On that note, let me debunk the limiting beliefs you have about your gratitude. You might think you have nothing to be grateful for. *You have an unbelievable amount to be grateful for.* I do not know your personal circumstances, but I know a few things: you have people who care for you in your life; you have qualities that serve the world; you have overcome challenges and hardships; you have the wonderful gift of life. As I will stress repeatedly in this book, that is not something to be taken lightly.

Perhaps you believe that gratitude will not provide a solution to your current challenges. Yes, gratitude is not a magic wand, but it does do something magical. Gratitude has allowed me to overcome my parents divorce, hating the way I looked, verbal and physical bullying, two mental health disorders and losing my Dad. I am not arguing with the magnitude of the pain your challenges have given you and are giving you, but I will guarantee that embracing gratitude will help you overcome that pain.

You may also have subscribed to the false belief that gratitude can only come when you're already happy, when you already have everything to be grateful for. This equation is the wrong way round. *Happiness doesn't create gratitude, Gratitude creates happiness.* When you live in constant gratitude, you will welcome whatever happens in life, you will always feel that you have enough, and thus you will always be happy. If you are ungrateful, you will never be satisfied with what happens in life, you will never feel that you have enough, and you will never be happy. There are plenty of healthy, attractive, rich, successful, adored and loved people checking into rehabs, taking anti-depressants and even sadly taking their own lives who demonstrate this point. We can have abundance in so many areas, but if we aren't grateful for it, then we won't be very happy.

So let me outline all the things we have to be amazed and inspired by. Let's see if you can pick out five of these things that you can be grateful for right now.

Body

- You possess 100 billion neurons in your brain, each of which possesses anywhere between 1,000 to 10,000 synapses. These neurons and synapses allow you to move, speak, see, smell, hear, taste, feel, learn how to play an instrument, draw and paint, play sports, dance, read books, laugh, feel happiness and love others. Whatever behaviour, thoughts and feelings you have right now, your brain is helping you to do it. Humans have the largest brain to body ratio of all the animals on Earth, without it we would not have found ourselves in the dominant position in our ecosystem.
- Your heart beats a 100,000 times a day. What else do you know that does something 100,000 times a day, all without a single command from yourself? The heart pushes 1.5 gallons of blood through more than 60,000 miles of blood vessels every *minute*. To put that in perspective, you have enough blood vessels in your body to circle the world twice. The record for a commercial flight completing this distance is 42 hours.
- When it comes to DNA, if you put all the molecules in your body together, they would reach the sun…and they would reach back again. And they would be able to do this another *600 times.* Also we share 98% of our DNA with chimps. If this small but significant change hadn't occurred, we would still be living in the jungle.

Environment

- Of all the people in history that have reached 65 years of age, half of them are living right now. We are blessed to have reduced the severity of many of our physical threats such as disease, natural disasters and famine.
- Trees are the perfect opposite to our lungs, both in shape and function. Without them we wouldn't have enough oxygen to breathe. We share a symbiotic relationship with them.
- The sun rises every single day to bring light and energy into our lives. When the sun dies, we have eight minutes left before we all die with it. We can be grateful that it continues to rise each and every day.

Technology

- In 1903 the Wright brothers flew for 59 seconds. 38 years later the Japanese bombed Pearl Harbour. 28 years after that, we landed on the moon. If someone from 200 years ago saw us coming out of a plane, they would think we were aliens or gods.
- You've got a smartphone in your pocket don't you? A couple of decades ago, if you wanted to make a phonecall, use the internet, check your diary, calculate a sum, take a photograph, get directions and play music, you needed *seven* different devices to do so. Your smartphone does all this and more.
- I may never have gotten this book to you without technology. The internet opened up the ability to self-publish and spread your message anywhere in the world. As I write this book I don't have the money to print thousands of copies and travel around the world distributing them. However, Amazon and Facebook have allowed me to spread my message to you.

Art and Literature

- The wisdom and works of past geniuses has been recorded for the rest of time in words and pictures such as *The Bible, The Mona Lisa, Hamlet* and the Hieroglyphs of the Great Pyramids. The meaning and value of these works is so complex, that we are still taking new perspective and understanding from them.
- The creation of *The Lord of the Rings, Harry Potter* and *Game of Thrones* has inspired and entertained billions of people. These works

have ignited creative expression and imagination in so many people. These stories have ingrained many important themes and values in our society such as choosing good over evil, the power of friendship and love, the virtues of courage and determination. It was reading Lord of the Rings and Harry Potter as a child that inspired me to be an author.
- Films and documentaries such as *The Day after Tomorrow, Blackfish, Philadelphia and Supersize Me* has raised awareness and action around important issues such as climate change, animal rights, AIDS, and diet. The medium of film can reach and move us in a way that many others methods don't.

Langauge

- In a 6 minute speech, Martin Luther King provided fresh inspiration and motivation to the Civil Rights movement, and improved the lives of millions of Black Americans. Martin was able to convey a vision that we could all understand and resonate with through the power of his words and voice.
- We are able to capture and express some of our most powerful concepts with a single word, such as "freedom", "love", or "life". The power of a single word can create connection and unity in people.
- Simple lyrics such as those in "Bohemian Rhapsody", "Candle in the Wind", "My Heart will Go On", "My Way" or "Stairway to Heaven" have to power to stir strong emotions and completely shift people's state.

Let's run through some of the research on gratitude, to see the magnitude of effects it can have on your life.

Dr. Martin Seligman conducted a study measuring various positivity tasks. Of all the interventions studied, asking participants to write a gratitude letter to someone who had never been properly thanked for their kindness, resulted in the greatest boost in happiness scores. This boost lasted for a month afterwards.

Professor Alex Wood and other colleagues measured students over a university semester and found gratitude levels were related to the students perceiving higher levels of social support and to lower levels of stress and depression, even when accounting for differences in personality.

Drs Robert Emmons and Michael E. McCullough measured participants over a ten week period. A third of the participants wrote at the end of each week what they were grateful for. A third wrote what had upset them. A third wrote about neutral events. Not surprisingly the gratitude group felt more optimistic and better about their lives than the other two groups. But more profoundly, this group exercised more and had fewer doctors visits than the other two groups, demonstrating how gratitude can impact our physical health.

So you can see that gratitude has some significant effects on our physiological and psychological state. As I alluded to at the beginning of this chapter, I believe gratitude is a key component of happiness, and I want to finish this introductory section by breaking some of the limiting beliefs you may have about happiness. Happiness is not something that is granted by luck. Your happiness is not determined by your genes and personality. Happiness is not something that you will find outside yourself. One of the best quotes I have ever heard in regards to happiness comes from Naval Ravikant:

"Happiness is Internal. It is a choice we make and a skill we develop."

Your happiness is entirely within your control. Yes, external events, experiences and people may make it easier to be happier or unhappier, but happiness comes from your decision to be happy. To pursue the things that make you happy regardless of external factors. The decision to practice gratitude on a regular basis is part of that pursuit.

On that note, I'm grateful that you've read this far! I'd like to now introduce you to my framework of how to make Gratitude a regular and positive part of your life. It is a three-part framework that you can remember through the acronym PPP: Physiology, Psychology, Practice.

Physiology

Let's look at what goes on in the body when we express gratitude. Gratitude, in its most basic form, can be a sigh of relief. We're grateful that cyclist just missed us, our team scored right at the end of the game, the person we asked out didn't say no. Gratitude serves to move us out of "fight or flight". When we're in a dangerous or stressful scenario, our body's defence mechanisms are ramped up: our hormone cortisol is released to increase blood pressure and blood sugar and suppresses the immune system. Our hormones epinephrine and norepinephrine (adrenaline) are released which accelerates our heart rate and breathing as well as impairing all non-emergency functions such as digestion, peripheral vision and even erections! This gives us vital strength and stamina when we need it, but it is taxing and tiring on our body.

Nowadays many modern scenarios and environments are putting us into "fight or flight", and this is where a lot of our negative physical and emotional health is coming from. Expressing gratitude therefore helps us press the "reset button" to return us to our default relaxed calm state. After a tough day at work, if one of the children is acting up or the car breaks down, expressing gratitude can provide relief to the fight or flight response.

Gratitude doesn't just help reverse negative physiological states, it helps enhance positive ones too. Grateful people have been found to report less aches and pains, exercise more (which activates a range of "feel-good" chemicals) and are more likely to attend regular check-ups. Research has found that expressing gratitude is linked with increases in our hormone DHEA ("anti-aging") and our IgA antibody (part of the first line of defence in our immune system). Gratitude makes us more aware of our health, and also generates physiological changes that actively have a positive benefit on it.

What I consider to be one of the most powerful effects of gratitude is that it releases Oxytocin, which can be seen as our "love hormone". Oxytocin is released when we hold hands, cuddle, engage in prayer and when we *give and receive* gratitude. Thus, expressing gratitude is an act of spiritual connection, and an act of *love*.

The most fascinating physiological effect that gratitude has, however, is that it synchronises our brain and heart rhythms. EEG (brain) and EKG (heart) monitors have observed individuals expressing gratitude until the two signals match. When this synchronisation occurs, our body is in its most optimal state for organs to carry out their functions, balancing emotions, and gaining mental clarity. You can achieve this through placing your hands on your heart, and "breathing into your heart". Spend two minutes breathing into your heart and focusing on three things you are grateful for, and you can synchronise your heart and brain, and achieve an optimal state of functioning.

Psychology

I believe that there is an important mindset shift that needs to be adopted in order to be able to truly cultivate gratitude. Stephen Covey in his book, *The Seven Habits of Highly Effective People,* highlighted the importance of shifting from the Win/Lose to the Win/Win mentality, and I agree. Let's outline the difference between these two mentalities, to understand how they relate to gratitude.

You see we've been brought up with a Win/Lose mentality. One child receives a C grade because another child received an A grade. One sports team loses because another team won. One postcode provides a lack of opportunity because another postcode hoards them all. From an early age we are taught to see that life is divided into winners and losers.

We then take this Win/Lose mentality into our careers and relationships. We believe that a win comes only with a loss. Naturally we would rather have the win, so we seek the win at the expense of someone else's loss. We become scripted by this Scarcity Mentality: that opportunities and resources are limited, and it makes us selfish and greedy. This is not our fault, it is just a result of how we have been brought up.

What Stephen asks us to develop is the Abundance Mentality. To realise that there is enough, and to be content with enough. When you develop this mentality, you shift out of Win/Lose. You don't fight and compete with the environment and people around you. You don't worry about and lament your position in life. If you feel you have enough (and more importantly feel that you *are* enough), then you do not see yourself as either a winner or a loser. You develop the Win/Win mentality. The recognition that whatever happens in life, you are always a winner, because you always have something to be grateful for.

This mentality brings about an important conception of the past. I want to outline to you a link between gratitude and blame. You can see them as opposites. One is a recognition for the positive things in your life, the other is a recognition of the negative things. Well what I challenge you to do is to recognise them as one and the same. You want to spread blame for what's gone wrong in your life? Then you'd better be prepared to spread blame for what has gone right.

We need to be grateful for the villains in our lives. The people, places and problems that have made our life a misery. You see everything that has happened in your life has shaped you into who you are now. The circumstances of your life have operated in line with a destiny to make you exactly who you were supposed to be.

Do you have a fear of failure because of over-demanding parents? Did someone screw you over and leave you broke? Did an illness permanently disfigure or impair you? Well blame these things, but blame them for everything.

Blame the parents who created the fear. Blame them for how they taught you to nurture and appreciate your children's achievements.

Blame the person who stole your money. Blame the person who put you on a new and prosperous career path because of your desperation for finance.

Blame the illness that you have to deal with every day. Blame it for making you more concerned about looking after your health and wellbeing.

I've done a lot of blaming in my life. Blaming the people who used to bully me at school. Blaming the education system for not teaching me important life skills. Blaming the cancer that took my Dad from me.

I blame those bullies for igniting my desire for personal transformation. I blame the education system for kindling my passion for teaching and service. I blame my Dad's cancer for teaching me the value of life and love.

See the thing is, a lot of us like to dish out the blame on a frequent basis. And despite this frequency, we're not even good at it! We miss out half the stuff we need to blame people and circumstances for. This is an important mindset shift that comes when you embrace abundance and

Win/Win. You are not just able to overcome the demons of the past, you are able to be grateful for them.

Gratitude doesn't just help you gain strength from the past, it allows you to find vibrancy in the rest of your life. Gratitude helps create a "positivity bias" in our present moment experience. As humans we are actually programmed with a default "negativity bias" whereby we more easily perceive and recall negative stimuli (and that's without the media feeding us stories of murder and war). Whenever we're in a challenging scenario, we can choose to find something we're grateful for, and focus our attention and energy on this positive stimuli. When we consciously self-regulate ourselves in this way, we gain the power to shift not just our present mood, but also to shift our long-term default position.

Neuroscience studies by Dr Richard Davidson have found that people with a higher level of positive feeling share a stronger link between their prefrontal cortex (our primary decision-making area) and a region of the brain called the Nucleus Accumbens (involved in motivation and reward). This exciting research has found that in these positive people stronger signals were sent from the prefrontal cortex to the nucleus accumbens, triggering feel-good neurotransmitter releases of dopamine ("reward" feeling) and endorphins ("high" feeling). What was also found was that positive people could actively control this link. The punchline? This suggests that we can, actually, *think ourselves happy*. When we take the active decision to find the positives in a situation, and be grateful for them, we are training this connection.

Practice

We've touched upon a couple of practices so far that you can use to train your gratitude muscle, but what I want to do now is outline more of my favourite and most effective practices than you can incorporate into your life to cultivate abundance.

Gratitude Journal

This was the first active practice of gratitude I introduced into my life, and it is still my favourite and most consistent. The premise is simple. At the end of each day, you write down three things you're grateful for. This can either be events or circumstances from that day (a smile from someone you fancy, an enjoyable exercise class, no traffic coming back from work), or wider things (fully working limbs, being married, living in a democratic country). Some days it will be easy to write three awesome things that happened, but the real value of the gratitude diary comes from finding gratitude in the small things. The recognition that no matter how stressful the day was, there were still things in it to be grateful for. This practice ensures that no matter the quality of the day, you go to bed with a "positivity bias", thinking of the things you were grateful for, not what you were ungrateful for.

This positivity bias has been shown to improve sleep quality in a Harvard Study, where it was confirmed that individuals who wrote in a gratitude journal before they went to bed experienced improved sleep quality. Additionally, Martin Seligman and colleagues conducted a study where participants were asked to keep a gratitude journal for one week. After this week, they demonstrated a 2% increase in their reported happiness. The participants had only been asked to record the journal for one week, but they felt so much benefit from it that they had continued. When their happiness was measured again after a month their scores had increased by 5% and by six months it was a 9% increase.

So get scribbling folks!

Gratitude affirmations

As well as finishing the day with gratitude, I like to start with it as well. As part of my morning routine I perform the heart exercise we talked about earlier, and I repeat something I'm grateful for 5 times, feeling that connection with my heart. I repeat this for two further things I'm grateful for. For those of you who really want to cultivate consistent gratitude, you can repeat such affirmations throughout the day. Set an alarm on your phone to go off every 3-4 hours, reminding you to take a quick couple of minutes to express your gratitude.

Gratitude Jar

If you are a more visual type, an excellent practice is to have a gratitude jar. Buy one of those big old-fashioned sweet jars and every day, write something to be grateful for on a slip of paper, and put it in the jar. Over time the jar will fill up, and whenever you're having a bit of a tough day, you can look at the jar and remember how much you have to be grateful for. You can even reach in and remind yourself of a specific thing to be grateful for.

The Oscar Speech

What does every single person do when they collect an Academy Award? They hold up that little gold figurine and rattle off all the people they're thankful for. The director, the producer, their agent, the make-up artists, their friends and family.

The Oscar speech is something we can do after we achieve something. After an accomplishment, take a quiet moment to yourself to give thanks to all the people who have made that possible for you. If you're feeling particularly creative, then gather those people in a room, hold aloft one of your garden statues and express that gratitude to them in person.

Food Gratitude

There are a number of food rituals based around gratitude: Burn's Night in Scotland, Thanksgiving in North America, saying grace before dinner. I've spent time in yogi communities and on meditation retreats, and one of the big lessons I've taken from these communities is their respect and love for living things. Part of their spiritual practice is to bring no unnecessary harm to a living being, as such these communities are usually vegetarian or vegan.

I will be honest and say their perspective has not stopped me eating animal products, but it has led me to appreciate the life on my plate. I remember and honour the life of any animal involved in my meal; whether that animal literally died, or gave up its life in captivity to provide me with butter or honey. I also remember that I'm incredibly fortunate to live in a country where we suffer no lack of food, and if anything our problems come from excess. So I have this little prayer that I say before consuming a meal.

"I would like to show appreciation to the (insert animal here) *who gave up its life to be a part of this*

meal. I would like to thank nature for providing me with these ingredients that sustain me, nourish me, and help me grow. And I would like to thank the universe, for providing me with an abundance of food."

I find this practice keeps me humble, and allows me to eat more mindfully and consciously. Try it even just once a day, perhaps during the family meal in the evening. Let's not Thanks-Give once a year, but 365 times a year.

Elaborate Thank-yous

I feel we say "thank-you" so flippantly nowadays, that it's lost a lot of its value. So I like to restore this value by giving elaborate thank-yous. This can be as simple as telling people fully and specifically how much you appreciate them and/or what they did. Imagine you hosted a party, and as your friend leaves they say "cheers buddy, great party". It's nice to hear, but doesn't really change your state. Instead, however, imagine that they said this:

"Mate I really needed this party. I had a tough week, and I needed the company and some fun to take my mind off it. That game of charades we played was hilarious, I loved your impression of Gandalf. You cooked some excellent food, I particularly liked the guacamole. Thank you so much for giving up your time and space to make this party happen, I really appreciate it."

That leaves you feeling a whole lot different doesn't it? (*Yes I've been perfecting that Gandalf routine for a while, and I paid special attention to getting that guacamole just right*). The level of appreciation here is so much deeper. Oxytocin is firing in both of you. That is the gift you can give yourself and others, just by taking a little extra time on expressing your thank-yous.

There are times you can take this a step further, through giving a gift. Here again try not to opt for the usual and obvious. Flowers, chocolates, cards etc are nice, but challenge yourself to go the extra mile, and buy something really specific to that person. It doesn't have to be big, because here the thought really does count. Is there a pastime or hobby you know someone loves? A treasured collection you can add to? Somewhere you can take them that you know they'll love. Examples of tailored gifts I've given have included a Teenage Mutant Ninja Turtle figurine, a tin of tuna and sweet chilli sauce, and taking someone to a Cat Cafe. You're probably wondering what kind of friends put up with me with these kind of gifts! But each of these gifts were tailored to a specific person for a specific reason, and thus you can't and shouldn't understand why I gave those gifts. Now I'm not suggesting you start dishing out the tins of tuna at Christmas to show people how original your gifts are! I'm using these as examples of the specificity to narrow down to, where only the person you gave the gift to could truly value that gift.

Expressing gratitude has a number of interpersonal benefits. Research has found that expressing gratitude to a new acquaintance makes them more likely to seek a long term relationship with you, and that grateful people display more prosocial behaviour such as increased empathy and reduced aggression. So seek to bring more gratitude into your relationships with others, and they can really prosper.

Gratitude Letter

An extension to the elaborate thank-you is a gratitude letter. This allows you to outline the full elaborateness of a thank-you to someone. I use this to sum up a relationship with someone. I have written gratitude letters to the flatmates I stayed with at university. I've written them to my best friends when I moved away from them. But the very first one I wrote was to Dad, when I had found out about his cancer. I outlined all the things I was grateful to him for, and what they meant to me.

Ideally, however, write someone a gratitude letter before they are about to die. Let them live a life where they understand how grateful you are for them, allow them to live with that good feeling. This is something you should spend a good couple of hours writing and honing. Whatever time you put into it will be magnified many times in the response of the person. And to remind you of the benefits on a more self-orientated level, writing a gratitude letter gives you a boost.

Remember the study conducted by Martin Seligman I described earlier? In his study measuring various positivity tasks writing a gratitude letter resulted in the greatest boost in happiness scores. A boost that lasted for a month afterwards. A study by Stephen Toepfer and Kathleen

Walker asked students to write three letters of gratitude to their friends over an eight week period. Their happiness was found to increase with each letter they wrote, demonstrating a cumulative effect of this practice. Sonja Lyubomirsky, one of the biggest researchers in the field of positive psychology (the study of happiness and flourishing), has found this benefit occurs even when you don't hand over the letter to someone. So if you're a little shy, just write or type down those thoughts (medium doesn't matter) and it will give you a boost.

With that understanding of the PPP system, I hope you now appreciate the outstanding effect on your life gratitude can have. It boosts our physical health, it changes our mindset, and it is so simple to begin to practice it regularly. I look back on Dad's death with an abundance of gratitude. I'm grateful for how he raised me. I'm grateful for the time we spent together. I'm grateful that I had the opportunity to spend the last 60 minutes with him. I'm grateful for all the lessons he was able to teach me through his death. I grateful for the passion and perspective I had developed since his death. Dad's death was incredibly painful, and it still brings me pain, but the gratitude I have overrides all that pain.

Questions and Activities

1. **The things I could be more grateful for are...**

2. **An aspect of my health that gratitude can improve is...**

3. **The times when I have defined myself as a winner or loser have been when...**

4. **I have been misattributing blame to...**

5. **The gratitude practice I think can really benefit me is...**

6. **Choose two gratitude practices, and implement them for the next 7 days. Evaluate how you feel after those 7 days.**

Chapter 4: Identity

"I'm incredibly proud to be your son"

I knelt down in front of the porcelain and took a deep breath. I had never done this before, but other people told me they did this all the time on nights out and when they were hungover. How hard could it be? I placed my index and middle finger together and thrust them to the back of my throat.

Urggh. The dry scrape of my fingers against the back of my throat was horrible. My eyes welled up and I felt a faint churn in my oesophagus. But the desired result didn't come. *I was going to have to do that again?*

I took another deep breath, wincing as the air whooshed over the part of my throat I'd just jabbed. I slid my fingers in with slightly more care this time and when they hit my gag reflux, I held them there and wiggled them slowly.

A sour eruption burst out my mouth and over my hand. That was the port and cranberry. My god it stung! I took my fingers out and repeated the manoeuvre. This time some of the ice cream came out. Each thrust of the fingers was like pushing a button on a time machine. I saw my meals come out in reverse chronological order. I jabbed at my throat until it was raw, tears streaming down my face and the acid of my stomach burning the entire passageway.

I flushed the toilet and slumped against the adjoining wall. I put my face in my hands and the tears flooded out.

That was a low point for me. I was having a flat christmas dinner and I had overindulged. I had gotten really drunk and lost my impulse control. I was so conscious and controlling of what I ate, when I ate, and how much I ate, but finally my body's burning desire for food had won out. I had stuffed myself, and a massive bowl of ice cream and jelly had gone down the hatch before I could stop myself. I freaked, and resorted to drastic measures.

That was the first time I had made myself throw up, and thankfully it was also the last. I had become so unhappy with who I was. I had been on a self-destructive path for months. Using alcohol to try an ignite a personality I was to afraid to express. Starving myself to change a body that I couldn't stand. Relying on caffeine to provide me with a superficial vibrancy that I was unable to generate for myself.

One of the underlying factors behind my eating disorder was a chronic dislike for who I was. What I looked like, how I spoke, what I did. My connection with my identity was weak. I was not connected with who I really was, and I couldn't connect with the false image I was trying to mould myself into.

Living our authentic identity is crucial to flourishing in life. Even if we are having a tough time with our health, work or relationships, having a strong identity gives us a firm bedrock through which to anchor ourselves. We are all seeking to know and understand ourselves, to establish ourselves in the various domains of our lives.

Understanding our identity provides us with a source of inner strength. I believe that within each of us is an incredible inner power. However, many of us have strayed away or failed to nurture this connection. So we search for that strong connection outside of ourselves: the way we look, who we know, the job we do. But our greatest power comes from the work we do within ourselves. I built up a crust around myself as hard as volcanic rock in my younger years, and every time I excavate a little further into this barrier I am invigorated by the rich ore I find beneath. The courage I am able to muster. The drive I am able to ignite. The love I am able to find. I have been astonished by the treasures I have found underneath, and I believe you too have a vast temple of treasures waiting to be discovered within you.

Connecting with our identity helps us align with our life's mission. When we start to understand our gifts, we understand why we're here. We start to appreciate the meaning of our presence here on Earth. A lot of us are wandering in life, trying to adhere to an identity that doesn't quite fit us. We're lost on the path because we shouldn't have walked that way in the first place. But when we reach a deep understanding of ourselves, the path becomes clear and we find we've had the map in our hand the whole time.

The best part of these discoveries, is the vibrancy through which we can live life. Feeling this inner strength and perceiving our mission infuses our life with energy, meaning and happiness. To be connected with our identity allows full and authentic expression. We live our truth. We live without fear, doubt, low self-esteem, anger, bitterness and sadness. Instead each of our actions burst with confidence, belief, passion, excitement and joy. Connecting with our identity allows us to connect with what is magical in life.

But I know what holds you back from this state of higher living. One of these blocks is we are scared of who we are. One of my favourite quotes comes from the film *V for Vendetta:*

"We wear a mask for so long we forget who we were underneath it".

We feel that connecting with ourselves ironically requires a period of *disconnect.* To detach from what we've known for so long. This uncertainty breeds fear. We hide parts of ourselves away in response to dramatic and traumatic events in our lives. We hide the aspects of ourselves that bring us shame, or don't get us what we want, or haven't helped us get to where we want to be. We treat these aspects of us like ex-lovers. We don't want them anymore in our lives, but we can't help but check up on them and reengage with them once in a while.

If you're scared of who you are, then I'm sad to say that you will be living in fear for the rest of your life. You can't hide from yourself. You can hide yourself from everyone else, but ultimately you'll always have to confront yourself. You might be scared of who you are, but only because that fear is a natural fear of the unknown. Because when you connect with yourself, you start to live authentically, and to live authentically is to live without fear. Do you know why that is? The root of the word "authentic" is "author", and it means to be the author of your own life. When you write the script for your existence, then there is no longer anything to be afraid of.

Another concern you may have is that even if you are connected with your authentic self, you don't have the confidence or self-esteem to express yourself fully. You don't have the knowledge or familiarity with this "new you" (which is really actually the "old you". Confusing isn't it?).

You are still scripted by all the barriers and habits you have created for yourself over the years. Being yourself actually feels unnatural. I can sympathise with that. I would constantly find myself in conflict between the actions of my old self and new self. I would struggle to adhere to the values that I wanted to live my life by.

What is required is to make the first step. In Psychology there is a process called the confidence-competence loop. This process describes how when we do more of something, we gain competence. When we gain more competence, then we gain more confidence. With that increased confidence, we then do that thing more. Learning to express yourself fully and authentically is no different. At first it will feel unusual and strange, especially if you've hidden it away for a long time. But as you express yourself more, you will get a little better at it, then you will get a little more confident at expressing yourself, and so you will engage in the confidence-competence loop.

Possibly our biggest fear is that by expressing who we really are, we will not be accepted by others and we will lose the acceptance of the people we already have in our lives. When it comes to not being accepted by others. Yeah you're right. People won't accept you.

But let me ask you this. Does everyone love you now? Are you accepted by everyone right now? Of course you're not. No one is. On the other hand, it's a fact of human nature that most people will accept you. Every time someone smiles at you, speaks with you, adds you as a friend on Facebook, sits next to you on a bus, holds open a door for you; they are accepting you. So would you rather live your truth and accept that a minuscule minority of people won't accept you…or would you rather hide from your truth and *still* have a minority of people not accept you?

What I've learnt in my life is that the people who matter accept you regardless, and the ones who don't didn't matter in the first place. When I underwent my personal transformation, I lost two friends. One as a result of my actions, the other as a result of theirs. But all the rest of my friends accepted my change. If anything they actually respected me more for it. They remarked on the positive changes I was making in my life, and even asked for advice on how they could make their own positive change. In fact I would not have found love with my partner if I hadn't stripped away the facade and started to live authentically.

On the note of love, I believe there is nothing more attractive than someone who is living their truth. That is the difference between someone who is beautiful and someone who is attractive. Attraction is all about personality. Someone who is living their authentic truth draws people like them to a magnet. That is why it is called ATTRACTion.

You're worried about not being accepted? Well people really respect someone who lives authentically. Again you won't be accepted by everyone. But you will be accepted by more people, and you're more likely to earn respect from those that don't.

Let's bring you out of the shadows, and let that light in you shine bright. The fuel for this fire is going to come from my ACE framework, which stands for Awareness, Cultivation and Expression.

Awareness

Finding the Gift

"Know thyself" the ancient Greek proverb decrees. I agree, which is why I suggest you start your journey of truth discovery with this life story exercise. I first did this when I was twenty years old and it radically shifted my perspective on my life. It brought me so much understanding and appreciation of exactly how I had gotten to where I was, and what I should look to do in the future. It pointed me towards the path of training and helping others, using my experiences to teach and guide people through their challenges.

This requires a heavy investment of your time, even if you only have a few decades to write about as I did. You don't just get out of this exercise what you put into it, you gain clarity which is more than worth the time invested.

There are several approaches to the exercise. To create time divisions: either you break your life into 5 year epochs (starting at 0-5), or into more subjective epochs (e.g. "school", "first job", "first marriage", "first child"). To analyse these chunks, you can either complete a chronological account of events, and then perform further analysis of each chunk, or you can analyse each one individually as you go. This is your exercise, so you are the best judge of what will work for you. Either way you will probably end up going through the exercise more than once to really grasp a firm understanding.

The basic premise is simple. You chart out the events, the challenges, the thought patterns, the relationships and the perspective that you had on the world during each epoch. Remember what you did, what you thought and what you felt. From each major experience identify what you learned, how you changed, and what strengths you developed.

As you start to go through this story, you will see a journey. In all our lives there is a story of Struggle, Solution and Success. We're all pretty familiar with our struggles. We've usually found solutions, yes sometimes they're dysfunctional, but we generally don't give ourselves appropriate credit for finding these solutions. From these solutions, we have then found success. This is something we definitely don't give ourselves enough credit for. Yes, it might not be the success we desire, or fit our definition of "success", but nonetheless we have it. A friend of mine defines success as "distance travelled", and by virtue of being able to look back and write about the past, you have achieved some distance and growth from your struggles. The reason I ask you to focus on learning, change and strengths is this demonstrates how you've grown.

When you have the full layout of your life story, you will start to notice themes and patterns running through it, and how all the events of your life connect. Whether positive or negative, it is not until we get this holistic view that these become obvious. We see scenarios where we have continuously excelled, understand the nuances of our relationships, the routines we have fallen into. When you begin to appreciate this holistic view, you are ready to complete the final section of the life story exercise.

For each of the epochs, get a sheet of paper and divide it into two columns: "Pain" and "Gain". Start in the Pain column, and write down all of your pain and suffering. Detail all the things that happened, all the hurt you were subject to. Have a damn good cry about it. You may be surprised about how much pent-up emotion there is to release. Next move across to the Gain column. Here list all your wins: your achievements; the strengths you've found; the positive people you engaged with; the new perspective you gained; the things you changed as a result of what happened.

It is important to appreciate that it doesn't matter if the columns are unbalanced; if you have more pain events than gains. The magic of this exercise comes from looking at your Gain column, grabbing yourself a luminous highlighter or glittery pen and colouring and identifying 1-3 of the biggest gains from that epoch. A person you met who is still in your life; a skill you learned that has brought you success or joy; a change in mentality that has made you stronger. This is the Gift. This is the present that you could gain only by experiencing this pain. This is a Gift that cannot be given, because to be given something is to not fully appreciate it's value. This is a Gift that has to be earned, and by God, you've earned it.

We talked about gratitude in the previous chapter, and when you see the gift of your struggles, you become grateful for them. I am grateful that I lost my Dad. I still miss him, and I would give a lot to have another day to spend with him, but I am grateful for what his death helped me become and achieve. There were so many gifts in my Dad's passing, and all these Gifts have helped me to write this book for you.

Meditation

The Finding the Gift exercise provides fantastic awareness, but it is not something we can do to regularly cultivate our personal awareness (although the life story exercise does benefit from occasional returns when fresh perspective and clarity occur). There are two regular practices that I have helped me acquire profound awareness and raised consciousness: the first is meditation.

Meditation has a ton of positive effects: reduced stress and emotional reactivity; improved concentration and memory; increased empathy and compassion. If there was medication that had the same effects as meditation we would all be taking it. Richard Davidson's research (remember his work on the link between the Pre-Frontal Cortex and the Nucleus Accumbens in the previous chapter?) has shown that meditation produces these effects by changing the structure of our brain. The areas of our brain related to executive functioning and positive emotion grow and develop.

Our cortex thickens and our nerves get more myelinated (meaning neural signals run stronger and faster). These are all fantastic effects, and each of them alone is reason to have a regular meditation practice. But I want to talk about what meditation does for our awareness.

First, let's break down some mental barriers you may have about meditation. It is not religious, it does not require any spiritual beliefs to gain benefit. You do not stop yourself thinking, that is impossible and no practitioner has ever managed to do so. You do not need to devote your life to it, as little as five minutes a day can bring benefit.

Here are five simple steps to start your meditation practice:

1. Set aside some time in a quiet space where you will be undisturbed for at least 20 minutes. This is a long enough period to allow yourself to shift your state and open up your consciousness, which is how we increase our awareness.
2. Sit in a chair with your hands resting in your lap, or lie on (not in!) your bed with your hands by your side.
3. For beginners I would recommend starting off with guided meditations (my friend Jason Stephenson has an extensive collection on his Youtube channel that I would highly recommend), then progress to using music without vocals (I use something called Binaural Beats, which is music tuned to the frequency of certain brain waves to help shift your neurological state).
4. Breath in through your nose, and out through your mouth. Envision cool, light air entering your body, and hot black air escaping. Breathe into your belly, not your lungs. This fully engages your diaphragm for deep, relaxed breathing.
5. Count your breaths. Each inhale is an odd number. Each exhale an even number. Count the breathes up to ten. When you get to ten, start again at 1. If at anytime your thoughts wander and you lose count, just start the process again at 1.

How simple is that? As you become more practiced in mediation, you can start to ask yourself questions. As a regular meditator, you will have strengthened the connection with your unconscious, your intuition, and the universe (however secular/spiritual you choose to conceive it. For me they all exist along the same pathway). You can pose questions to this connection, and start to receive answers back.

Now don't get freaked out, this is not like having a conversation! This is akin to getting an "aha" moment, a feeling of deja vu or knowing what someone is about to say before they say it. It is a moment of inspiration or increased consciousness. It doesn't happen immediately, sometimes not even that day. All you are doing is posing a question to a deeper part of yourself. You have to give it the appropriate amount of time to process it, as any problem requires a proportional amount of time to find a solution. I may ask for guidance on a specific issue or decision, but every day I will ask "Universe, what would you have me do today?". You can use whatever language you are comfortable with, but this question primes your inner tutor (wonder why it's called "in-tuition"?) to guide your actions that day, and steer you towards acting as your highest self.

Coaching

My second regular awareness practice is receiving coaching. I provide coaching as part of my services, but like any good coach I also receive coaching. Coaching is based on the old proverb: "two minds are better than one". Some of you may have less than fond memories of sports coaches blowing the whistle and making you do laps. Coaching for personal development is not like that. It is simply having a sounding board and guide to help you find the answers you already know. You combine the processes of your two minds to identify solutions and unearth inner power.

Now, as a coach myself, of course I am going to tell you about how wonderful coaching is! However, the reason that I talk about coaching is because I want to acknowledge the people who have coached me. My Dad of course was my coach, and I have been blessed to cross paths with other individuals who have nurtured my development (shoutout to you guys in the acknowledgements section). I am passionate about coaching because I know how life-changing it can be. A good coach will help accelerate your growth process and help you discover parts of you that you didn't know you had.

I would love to be your coach, but make sure you hire *someone* as your coach. Life coaches are good, but there are also very specialised coaches out there (examples I have met include passion coach, writing coach and even sex coach!). If you are particularly aware of an area of your development you would like to explore and learn more about, see if you can find a coach for it.

Cultivation

Once we have found awareness of ourselves - who we are, what we stand for and what we seek to be - we can seek to build our identity. We stake our claim on who it is we project into the world, and what we want to achieve. The founding fathers of the United States did this on the grounding of a constitution, and that is exactly what you are going to do too.

Personal Constitution

Your personal constitution decrees the type of person you want to be, and what you are going to create. This statement sets the foundation for how you wish to live your life. The constitution is created by writing two documents.

The first is your values statement. What are the key components of who you are? What are your strengths? What qualities do you wish to put forth into the world? Start by identifying your main values (e.g. mine are Positive Mindset, Authenticity, Drive, Love and Leadership) and then identify the sub values that contribute to that value (for Positive Mindset mine are power of thought, gratitude, optimism and hope, learning from pain). Take some time over this. Write out examples of how you are going to express those sub values. This is a vision for how you want to live and express yourself every day. It should be a document of at least a couple of pages, and it deserves to have some time invested in it.

When you have completed that long-form statement, store it somewhere safe so you can refer to it on occasion. Now complete a one page summary of your value statement. Highlight your Main Values (In a single word if possible) and summarise the sub values that lead to them in bullet point form. Then stick this one page summary somewhere you will see it everyday, that could be your bedroom wall, in front of your desk or even on the fridge. This is a constant primer and reminder for the standards you set yourself.

You then create your purpose statement. What do you want to create? Who are you going to influence? What is your life's mission? How are using your Life Story Gifts to serve the world? Identify your main purposes and again identify the sub-purposes that will contribute to that main purpose (For example, one of my main purposes is to constantly cultivate growth, and the sub-purposes that contribute to that are challenge, self-awareness, adventure and spontaneity, and meeting like-minded people). Again these are the things that are going to make your life mean something, so spend some time writing down a couple of pages. Then again, create that one-page summary and stick it alongside your value statement.

It's important to note that these statements are not intended to be set in stone for life. Just as the American Constitution has amendments, so will yours. This is a natural part of growth. However, the statement provides the foundations on which to build this growth. Thus it is important to consistently monitor how you are sticking to these values and purposes. This can be achieved through journaling.

Journaling

My second cultivation task is journaling. I sometimes feel I have a journal for everything! There's a gratitude journal, business ideas journal, emotional wellness journal, creative journal and self-reflection journal; and it's that final one I want to discuss with you now. This is a journal that you complete at least weekly (the best in the business do it daily). In this journal you record the key events that happened that week, who you interacted with, what challenges you faced, the achievements you made, which lessons you learned. You can view the journal somewhat as a small version of the life story exercise.

You reflect on each of these domains, what went right and wrong, what was lost and gained, what was interesting, novel and exciting. The key difference is that the journal is a little more future orientated that the life story exercise, the journal is written with the intention of building for the future.

After writing my journal, I look at the description and write down take-home points: what lessons I've learned and perspective I've gained. These are things that I want to make myself more self-aware of.

For example, did I fail to be fully authentic in a key interaction that week? Was I less in control of my thought patterns than I'd like to be? Were my self-care routines not on point? This is awareness that I can then take into the next week and seek to be more authentic, positive and disciplined. It is important to also write about what is going good for you: how did you enhance an interaction, rise above negativity, or focus yourself? These are also practices to be self-aware of and continue to hone and cultivate in the future. That is the value of the journal, it provides a source of constant evaluation to clarify and hone your development.

Learning

Journaling is a specific example of what I consider to be an overall practice vital to cultivating your growth: learning. When you learn you strengthen and develop your core values, and enhance your skills and abilities. On my value statement there are numerous components related to learning; allow me to share some of my favourite methods of learning.

Every day I read books and listen to podcasts from the top experts in my field. The joy of my business is when I'm studying for it, I learn great life skills. Conversely, when I learn great life skills, that translates into material for my business. I would recommend that you digest books and podcasts related to what you're passionate about and your personal development every day (luckily for me they're the same thing!).

I safeguard the time before I go to sleep for reading. I would strongly urge you to read books, rather than read online. Reading online creates the temptation for distraction, and can also feel that it's not a disconnect from work, as we often do so much work on computers. Reading a book gives you an opportunity to be mindful, and to ease yourself away from distractions.

Additionally, a book is still the most popular and powerful way that people share their message. If anyone has something worth saying, they put it in a book (exhibit A right here). You get the dissected wisdom of highly successful and interesting people at a very low price point. The world's second richest man, Warren Buffet, reads for 6-8 hours every day. I think that is the biggest testimonial I can provide as to the benefit that reading can bring to your life.

Podcasts are another favourite of mine. We have so much dead time in the day: commuting, waiting for people, driving and walking places. This is time I like to fill up by listening to podcasts. Podcasts are one of the fastest growing forms of communication, and they are FREE. Again you get a direct connection with the thoughts and teachings of some of the world's most interesting and successful people. If reading is something you struggle with, then podcasts provide a great supplement/alternative.

A third practice I seek to do for my daily learning is connect with others. I don't mean to exchange small-talk with them, but to learn something from them. Other people are such a valuable source of learning. It is through asking others questions and hearing their stories about the world that allows us to rapidly expand our consciousness. That is why I argued in an earlier chapter for an international service program. The more diverse the range of people you meet, the faster and deeper your learning. Asking people questions about what they think and feel and how they see the world can really broaden your insight and perspective.

As well as meeting new people, I also think it is essential to spend time with like-minded people. People who share your values, beliefs, vision and interests. Spending time with such people is great for cultivating our identity, because it makes it easier for us to be authentic and expressive. With these people we can explore ourselves so much deeper. We feel comfortable doing so because we know we are with people who are sympathetic and understanding to the work we are attempting to do. The depth that you can go to with such people is extraordinary, and it leads to some fantastic inner work.

Expression

That last point leads nicely into the third part of the A.C.E framework. When we have nurtured and reconnected with our identity, we then need to become comfortable expressing it. I believe that the key to a more harmonious and prosperous society is to have more people expressing their full, vibrant selves. Too many people are living in a shell, keeping themselves hidden away from the world. Many people confuse expressing themselves with imposing themselves. Expressing yourself doesn't mean trying to take over conversations or swaggering around with ego. It just means embracing and sharing your true self, and I have three techniques to help you do so.

Self-Affirmations

Affirmations are something that I feel the self-help field has sadly given a bad rap. It's all about repeating positive affirmations to yourself over and over again. "I am a billionaire". "I am popular and famous". If you say it enough times then it will become reality.

Not so. Affirmations such as these are lies, and your subconscious knows they are lies, and will actively fight them. Positive affirmations such as these have actually been found to have negative effects, not positive ones, leading to demotivation and lowering self-esteem. The very opposite effect of what they are supposed to achieve!

However, affirmations do have their place, and are effective at shifting your state and affirming what you want. However, what should be practiced is self-affirmations. This is where you affirm something you already have, not something you want.

To create an affirmation, you need three criteria, which you can remember through the acronym PDP. First it is Personal, so you say "I", and you affirm a value or quality that you actually have. Secondly, it needs to make a strong Declaration such as "I can", I show", I create". Thirdly it is Positively-Charged, so you focus on addition, not subtraction. So you would not say "I will not lose my temper today", you would say "I can remain calm today". When you focus on things in the negative, you actually prime that negative outcome in your mind.

Each morning I pick three values from my value statement that I want to affirm, and I make an affirmation based on my existing qualities using the PDP framework. For example for Positive Mindset I might use the affirmation "I constantly seek the gratitude in every situation" or "I have hope and optimism for what I can achieve in the future". I will repeat that affirmation 5 times (shout it if you don't have anyone you will wake up or disturb) and do so again for two other values.

By doing this, you are calling your highest self into action. Importantly, you are not trying to manifest some false self. You are priming your conscious and unconscious mind with a reminder of what standards you expect of yourself, and the importance of what you're working towards.

Vulnerability

A massive step towards expressing yourself is to allow yourself to be vulnerable. Remember that fear we talked about at the start of the chapter? The fear of being judged? We face and overcome that fear through vulnerability. We put our authentic self on the table, we let people see exactly who we are and what we've got. We throw away the mask and liberate our identity.

The first part of vulnerability comes through ownership. You own your fears, you own your struggles, have pride in where you've been and what you've overcome. You appreciate the gains that have come from your life story. Throughout this book I have told you about my struggles: being a fat kid who was bullied, having a terrible dating record, my mental health issues. It was not easy the first time I told those things to people. Yet I have been encouraged by the amount of acceptance I have experienced. By continuously being vulnerable with my pain, I've taken ownership over it. I speak about my struggles at my talks, networking events, conversations with my friends. These things no longer have any power over me, because I took ownership.

I'm not saying you immediately start telling everyone about your deepest fears and traumas, but you can start by taking ownership of them. Write down a painful experience from your past, and after it write "I take ownership of you." Feel the freedom and power that comes from that simple act. Repeat the process for all the other baggage you are carrying around with you. This is a task that you may want to add on to the Finding the Gift exercise.

The second part of vulnerability is standing by beliefs and values. When we have a strong opinion on something, there is inevitably someone who will have a contrasting opinion. Now the problem we have in society right now is we're scared of debate and freedom of speech. We like freedom of speech, but only when it agrees with our freedom of speech. People are criticised on a chronic level if they stand out nowadays. The advent of the internet has sadly increased the breadth and depth of criticism. The trolls and armchair critics have more reach with their poison. As a result of this, we're often scared of giving our opinion, we're scared of what the repercussions might be. It's okay to have opinions; opinions keep things interesting and it's the only way to get things done.

Having an opinion can be scary, and it can lead to a lot of conflict. Martin Luther King had an opinion. He believed that people shouldn't be judged based on the colour of their skin, and many people hated him for it. Winston Churchill had an opinion that Hitler was very dangerous, and most people didn't take him seriously. Galileo had an opinion that the Earth was not the centre of the universe, and he was ostracised by society for it.

But each of them didn't let their critics stop them from expressing their opinions. And what happened? They changed people's opinions! Forty five years after Dr. King told the world he had a dream, America elected its first black President. After years of telling the government to do something about Hitler, Winston Churchill was elected Prime Minister. For centuries after Galieo's death, astronomers and scientists continue to explore and expand upon his observations. That is the power of having an opinion: you might just make a difference in the world.

Creation

Creation is our most powerful vehicle for expression, even more so than language. You were creating and imagining things long before you could talk. Creation is what we put into the world, it is the mark we leave after we are gone. Creativity is how we express ourselves. When you draw, sing, dance, weave, paint, stitch, rap, cook, dress or write, you are being creative, and through this creativity, you are expressing yourself.

So let me ask you this...are you creating something every day? Because if you aren't, then you aren't fully expressing yourself. And no the emails you write at work don't count. That awkward shuffle you do in the nightclub doesn't count. Your Mac *a la* Cheese for dinner doesn't count. I'm talking about things that really contain your spirit and passion.

What hobbies and pastimes really engage you? Whether that is writing scripts or collecting stamps, do more of that. What activities or pursuits do you highly value? Have you considered blogging or teaching that discipline? What causes or needs really fire you up? Perhaps you could create or join a community project related to this? Whatever it is, make sure it is something that is aligned with who you are, and this makes it incredibly easy to add your input, because all it requires is your full, authentic self.

This book has been simple to write. Yes, there have been times when I've had to think about structure or nail down my research, at the end I will have to edit and proofread. These things are an effort. But the raw communication of this book has flowed from me. Writing this book has felt so in touch with who I am and what I want to express and create, getting words on the page has been the easiest part. I have found full, authentic expression in this writing, and it has made me feel so alive. If you can find that level of expression in your lives, you'll feel pretty alive too.

Questions and Activities

1. **The Masks I wear or Personas I adopt in my life are…**

2. **The biggest fear I have about living authentically is…**

3. **After analysing myself, I am more aware of…**

4. **The qualities I wish to cultivate are…**

5. **If I express myself more fully, the benefits I will feel are…**

6. **Pick two strategies from this chapter to implement over the next 7 days. Evaluate how you feel after these 7 days.**

Chapter 5: Love

"I love you Dad"

I can't remember what I want to tell you. I can't remember the time when love hurt me the most. When Dad and Mum got divorced, the event was so painful for me, I cannot even remember it…an early defence mechanism. I remember us all living together in the same house, and then I remember living in two different homes. I know at some point I must've been sat down and told the news, but I cannot remember it. I guess you can't remember something you don't fully comprehend, because my four-year-old self couldn't fathom how his two role models could no longer love each other. Yes, I remember the arguments; yes, I remember the tears - but I guess I thought that was normal.

This experience scarred me deeply. It was an isolating experience. I had no brothers or sisters for comfort and support; nobody who understood what I was going through and who I could confide in. I had half-siblings from Dad's first marriage (my old man was a great dad but a poor husband!), but they were all grown-up and living elsewhere. Mum and Dad were both incredibly supportive, but inevitably they could only give me a biased interpretation of the situation.

It also made me feel like an outcast at school. This might sound surprising given the current prevalence of separated parents, but divorce wasn't that common in my hometown at that time, and certainly not when I first entered school (although many of the "happy families" I envied did split at a later date). I was the only one in my class with divorced parents for the first three years of school. My classmates couldn't understand it, and it always made me feel like there was something wrong with *me*.

The most traumatic aspect of the divorce though was being taken away from my mum. This may come as a surprise to you, given that this book is about my dad, but my mum was the parent I was most attached to for the first decade of my life, and certainly at that age. I missed her terribly. My mum had to do shift-work at the airport to support herself and me, so Dad decided that he should take chief custody. He looked after me during the week, and I saw Mum at weekends. Every time she drove me back to Dad's it felt like I was losing her again. The mother-child bond is a unique and special one, and this bond was cut for me at an early age, and I had to suffer through the pain of having it cut week after week.

Harry Harlow did a famous psychology study in the '60s. The study was designed to measure what creates the infant-caregiver relationship. The predominant opinion at the time was the "cupboard theory", which suggested that the relationship was developed through feeding. Harlow investigated by separating young Resus monkeys from their mothers at birth, and providing inanimate "surrogate mothers". One was a wire frame with a milk bottle. The other was a wire frame wrapped in cloth. The young monkeys overwhelming chose the cloth-covered mother. They craved comfort and connection more than physical sustenance.

One of the biggest findings of Harlow's studies was the long-term psychological effects of removing the infants from their mothers. These monkeys were reclusive, showed a poor understanding of social games and interactions with other monkeys and also demonstrated heightened aggression.

I endured similar psychological trauma. I always just seemed "different" from other kids. I could never understand their games; I always seemed to make a fool of myself; I was always an easy target for bullying and teasing, because I never fought back. The divorce was so incomprehensible and painful for me, and at that early age I had not developed the emotional capacities to properly process it. So my innate psychological defence mechanisms kicked in, and I internalised everything. Anything that caused me pain and discomfort I pushed deep into my unconscious mind.

I never reacted and never responded to any negative input. I talked with Dad about this shortly before he died and he said: "I could see that you were trapped inside yourself. Sometimes I would be telling you off and shouting and screaming at you and you just stood there, like a stone statue".

I can trace all the struggles in my life back to this separation. Love hurt me, so I made the early, immature decision to live without love…and look where it got me. For the next two decades there was a hole in me that was never filled, and this emptiness materialised in numerous unpleasant states of suffering. When we live without love, we live an empty life.

You see, ironically, love is what would've released me from the pain and hurt I had experienced. Remember we talked about our hormone, oxytocin, in the chapter on gratitude? Oxytocin is also released by acts of love, especially through human touch. Now oxytocin doesn't just make us feel warm and fuzzy, it actively shuts down our stress and pain responses. When a child falls and scrapes themselves, what do they do? They run and hug their mum and get a kiss to make it better. This isn't just some childish ritual, it provides biological relief. That touch and kiss pumps oxytocin into the child's system, and shuts down their feeling of pain. That is a microcosm of how love can diminish our pain and suffering.

Love is what allows us to understand and relate to others. Love is what attracts us to each other and give respect to each other. We need an intense, powerful feeling to keep us engaging with each other. That feeling is love. A very crude analysis, but at the primal function level that is what it does. At a higher level though, it opens us up to each other. It enhances our perspective and deepens our knowledge. The people that you can be most open and expressive with are those who you love. Love is the bridge that allows you to connect the distance between you and exchange parts of yourself with each other. The trust and faith we place in love helps us to create our happiest experiences together.

Love provides existential guidance for our lives; when we have a decision to make, the decision based on love provides the greatest dividends. As a human race we continuously take steps towards love, not hate. Yes, we've done a tragic amount of killing each other, but love has been the more consistent character in our narrative: there have been more marriages in our history than wars, more families than military battalions, more practitioners of religion than practitioners of murder.

The inroads we are making on the front of international relations and equality represent a progress towards love, not away from it. Being in love and feeling love provides a meaning for our existence and makes us want to contribute to the world. The greatest creatives, scientists and leaders have undertaken their work due to a thorough caring and love for their fellow human beings: a desire to add to and benefit their lives.

However, as the atrocities of human existence and the trauma of our personal lives highlight, love is not always so easy to embrace. Let's look at some of the reasons why you may have moved away from love, or feel scared of it.

One of the most common reasons is that a loving experience has hurt you: you lost someone you love. I know that pain. My parents' divorce, a girlfriend leaving me for another guy, losing my Dad, these experiences hurt like hell. It leaves you in a state of despondency unlike any other. However, it is not love that hurt you. You see love does not hurt us, ever. All love ever does is heal us and energise us. Love never takes away, it only adds.

What gets hurt is our ego. Our self-concept takes a separation personally, it sees this separation as a threat to our survival. If we lose love, we lose security, comfort, company, confidence, self-efficacy, identity and a host of other important constructs which make up the human condition: or at least that is how our ego makes us see it. This is what we see ourselves losing, and indeed we can lose grasp of these things. *But we never lose love.* We never lose the capacity to care for and connect with others.

However, when the ego is really hurt, it can block us from caring and connecting. When we suffer an intense emotional wound, the brain will block off and take away attention from the emotion that caused this wound. This is a defence mechanism to reduce pain. However, this is a nuclear option. This mechanism blocks all feeling. If you've been hurt too many times in life, you may struggle to connect with feeling again, because your brain has performed a mass shutdown. Some individuals find themselves spending months or years engaging in therapy to try and press the reset button on this nuclear neurological shutdown. It took me over 15 years to start opening myself up to feeling again after my parent's divorce.

Another limiting belief you may have is that you have no one to love. You've been searching for the one, but never found them. There is no one who quite matches you. You've spent a lot of time in unfulfilling relationships, and you're fed up searching.

Are you kidding? How big is your sample size? 5? 10? 50? Maybe it's even a 100. Whatever it is, it's insufficient. There are 7,000,000,000+ people in the world, and you're giving up after trying to bond with less than 0.00001% of them? Would you quit a marathon after running the first couple of metres? I would complete an *ultra-marathon* if it brought me love.

If you are thinking this way, it's likely because you've fallen for the Hollywood myth that love is meant to be, that it blossoms naturally and everyone lives happily ever after. However, the stories never tell you that "happily ever after" is just the beginning. Love has to be worked on. Love has to be cultivated. Love is a feeling but it is also a skill, and like any skill it requires appropriate dedication. My partner and I have great chemistry, but we also have to work hard at our relationship. We have to work hard to maintain that feeling and the standards of the relationship we wish to uphold. We work hard at continuously opening up and deepening the connection and bond between us.

What can be the most ingrained and poisonous belief, is that we are not worthy of love. This usually comes from our early environment or upbringing, and it can haunt people for the rest of their lives. This is a hard poison to expunge, and I won't claim that there is any hard and fast relief. But what I will say is that if you feel this way, I want to tell you that you are a unique and remarkable being, and I believe you deserve to be loved. Every human deserves love. We are born as loving beings. Look at the way a baby looks at people, that is love. That is an individual who has not yet been tarnished and broken by the lack of love from others. That love is at the core of your soul, and there will be many people who want to connect with that love. What I hope we can achieve together in the rest of this chapter, is to open you up to that love.

Because love is always worth it. Yes, I lost my Dad, and I lost the opportunity to express love with him. But it was still worth spending those twenty-two years of love with him, and his love didn't die with him. I hold that love with me. It will be with me for the rest of my life, and I will give it to others the way he gave it to me. Writing this book is an act of love, which has been inspired by my Dad's love.

As I said, love is a skill. It is something we train and develop. Through the following strategies, I hope to help you design a life that attracts more love. Allow me to outline the three "Ls" of Love: Letting Go, Listening, and Lavishing.

Letting Go

Conflict is the antithesis of love. Whether that be inner conflict or conflict with others, we need to resolve that conflict to clear the channels that allow us to fully feel and express love. This is achieved through forgiveness, for ourselves and others.

In order to open ourselves up to love, we first need to be comfortable with our own faults. We direct a lot of criticism and negativity towards ourselves. We say things to ourselves that we would never let anyone else get away with telling us. I hope that the life story exercise from the previous chapter has allowed you to recognise that you have many fine qualities and achievements that deserve praise. You may still, however, be harbouring some resentment and blame for yourself. This will block the pathways through which you receive love. Let's run through an exercise to release some of this negativity you may be feeling.

It's pen and paper time again. We're going to be writing a letter to very important person: you. Specifically a younger version of yourself. Focus on an event that causes you to devalue yourself. Begin by addressing the letter to yourself and listing the things that went wrong, the people that were hurt, the issues it caused. Be honest and blunt with this. List all your transgressions, real or imagined. Because after you've listed each point, you're going to write: "For this <insert your name>, I forgive you" on a separate line. I'll run through an imaginary example.

Dear Blank,

Your alcoholism wrecked your body. You impaired your brain functioning. You caused yourself a number of serious injuries through drunken acts. You had to get a liver transplant. You nearly killed yourself.

For this Blank, I forgive you.

You were a brute to those who loved you. You ignored your friends. You were aggressive towards your wife. You scared your children. You hurt everyone close to you.

For this Blank, I forgive you.

You wasted so much potential. You lost a great job due to your addiction. You abandoned your dreams. You spent day after day searching for happiness at the bottom of the bottle, instead of seeing the opportunities for happiness that were all around you.

For this Blank, I forgive you.

After you have completed this section, you solidify the forgiveness. After you have stated your forgiveness, you then summarise why you are forgiving yourself. You may choose to list all the lessons you have learned from that experience. You may accept that everyone makes mistakes, and everyone deserves their chance at redemption. If you feel none of these things, then here is what you can write (and in fact everyone should write this as their concluding sentence).

I forgive you <insert your name>, because I want you to move on with your life. The past has already happened, there is nothing you can do to change it. I know you would like to change it, and because of this, I forgive you. You deserve to move on, and create a new future for yourself. I give you this gift of forgiveness to allow you to do so.

Equally, you may have a huge amount of resentment and blame directed towards others. We must let go of this too. When we fail to forgive someone, we have allowed them to hurt us twice. Once through their behaviour, and twice by allowing their negativity to continue to affect our lives. This will block the channels through which you wish to give and receive love.

You can write a letter to them in the exact same way. Listing all of the ways they hurt you, real or imagined, and each time saying you forgive them. All that changes is the summary paragraph. Accept their mistakes, express hope for their redemption and healing. If you can't find this in your heart, then just tell them you are writing the letter for your own peace of mind. Looking something like this:

I forgive you <insert their name>, because I want to release this pain. The past has already happened, I accept nothing can be done, and it's time to move on. I believe you have a chance for redemption. I hope you find the healing you require. I forgive you. I deserve to move on, and create a new future for myself. I give you this gift of forgiveness to allow me to do so.

The more compassion you can show someone, the more powerful this exercise will be. However, I know all too well that this is not always possible. I had someone in my life whose actions I just could not fully forgive: I had hope for their redemption, but I could not feel compassion for them. I'm sure someone on a higher spiritual plane than myself could. However, I'm not at that stage. I think it's okay to accept that. It takes courage to accept your limitations. You offer all the forgiveness and good intention you can, then seek to move on.

In this particular example I did something ceremonial, which helped me let go slightly better, and may help you let go more. Once you have written this letter, burn it. I took mine outside and ran a lighter across it; you may have a barbecue or fireplace to burn yours in. The act of burning is transformative. The paper becomes ash, fumes are released, and you'll never see that letter again. Your resentment becomes forgiveness, the negativity is released, and you'll never let that circumstance rule you again.

Listening

Love stems from an appreciation of another. And how can we appreciate others if we do not understand them? I believe a lot of the relational problems outlined in my introductory chapter have been caused by people not seeing each other's perspectives. We need to learn about this perspective in order to begin to form a connection with them, and this learning begins with Listening.

Listening is a poorly taught and poorly practiced skill. Think back to school. All those years that were spent teaching us how to read, how to speak, and how to write. But who ever taught us how to listen? We never had Listening 101.

So all too frequently we impose ourselves in conversations, putting across our point of view, our concerns, our stories, without appropriate consideration for the other person. This is not our fault, it's not because we don't care or are not interested, it's because of the way we've been taught. So we have divorce rates at 50%, we have politicians riding on a wave of xenophobia and intolerance and we have war between religions.

This is what Sir Alex Ferguson, one of Sport's greatest coaches and team leaders has to say on listening. "There's a reason God gave us two ears, two eyes and one mouth. It's so we can listen and watch twice as much as we talk". In my work I summarise this as the 49% rule. In interactions we should seek to speak no more than 49% of the time, which means that our number one behaviour in interactions is always listening.

As part of my preparation for becoming a coach, I did a year of counselling training. One of the key tenets we talked about was Validation, and that is essentially what you give a person by listening to them. The reason why therapy works is because, for what can be the first time in someone's life, they feel that someone respects and understands their position. This is what a person feels when they believe someone is truly listening to them.

Here is a phrase that will allow you to give everyone you speak to that validation. In his book *The 7 Habits of Highly Effective People*, Stephen Covey asks us to "Rephrase the Content and Reflect The Feeling". The reason why this approach works is twofold. In order to rephrase the content, you have to have heard what the person said in the first place. That is always a good start!

Secondly, in order to reflect the feeling, you need to have an element of empathy. A person will rarely say "I feel angry" or "I feel sad". To identify the underlying emotion, we require this empathy. A psychopath would have no problem rephrasing the content, but they lack the empathy to be able to reflect the feeling. If there is no emotion and no empathy, then there is no human connection.

So let's look at how this plays out. Imagine a friend comes up to you and opens up: "I'm trying to lose weight and nothing is working". Here are four possible responses.

1. Repeat the Content: "You're trying to lose weight and nothing is working"
2. Rephrase the Content: "You feel you're overweight"
3. Reflect the Feeling: "You sound frustrated"
4. Rephrase the Content and Reflect the Feeling: "You sound frustrated at feeling overweight"

Can you see the difference between these statements? Repeating the statement back to the person is annoying and doesn't help them. Rephrasing the content alone is likely to get a short Yes/No answer, but it shows you're listening at least. Then do you see how reflecting the feeling requires that touch of empathy? They did not say they were frustrated or use any synonym of frustrated, but I'm sure we can agree that this person is frustrated.

But the magic happens when we show that we've been listening and display that empathy. With the statement "You sound frustrated at feeling overweight" you open the person up to agreement and expansion. They will then begin to tell you more about how they are feeling, and perhaps ultimately why being overweight is such a trigger for them. Each time they provide information, you can use the same technique to delve deeper and deeper.

The best thing about this technique is that this works even when you know it's being used on you! When I'm on the receiving end of coaching, I'll hear my feelings being reflected and validated, but it still makes me feel good, and still helps me to solve my problems. So in future interactions, peg back on your chatter, and run through this procedure when someone is telling you something important about themselves.

Listening is a powerful tool for collecting information about people. However, understanding is not something we want to passively collect, but proactively seek. The way we minimise our talking and maximise our learning is by asking questions. There is only so much we can learn and experience by ourselves in our lifetimes. But we can open ourselves up to billions of other sources of knowledge and experience by asking others about their lives.

I'll give you an example that came the night before I wrote this section. I was at a networking event and I was speaking to a school teacher. As it was a business event, I asked her what her interests in this area were. She began telling me that she had spent some time travelling in South America, notably the Galapagos Islands, and that she wanted to start a business hosting bespoke, tailored tours there.

Now how interesting is that? How many people do *you* know who have visited the Galapagos Islands? For most of us that's a list of one - Charles Darwin - but he's not around any more to tell us about the experience. I found out about the wildlife, the culture and the language (yes the Galapagos Islands are inhabited, I didn't even know that!). To get that experience myself I would have to save a lot of money and time to travel halfway round the world. Instead with one question I opened up a fascinating account that had me truly engaged with this individual.

What's more I felt I had a deep understanding of this lady. I could hear her enthusiasm, feel her passion, and see her vision. There was love there. Not sexual or romantic love, but a spiritual love. A love of an individual who was so connected to her life's mission. I was moved and educated by it. Would I have got that if I just pitched my work and forced my business card in her face like so many people do at these kind of events?

You see something very special happens when humans swap stories like this. A 2010 study at Princeton discovered that when you tell a story, certain brain regions linked to emotion are activated. Nothing too surprisingly there. However, it has been found that when someone listens to that story, the exact same brain regions are activated in *their* brain.

Thus when you listen to someone's story, not only are you learning, *you are synchronising your brain with that person*, and that helps develop a powerful connection between the two of you.

That perhaps explains that feeling of love I felt. This lady was speaking about something she loved, and her emotional centres were firing like crazy, and my emotional centres were synchronising with hers.

In order to be able to do good listening, we thus also have to ask good questions. Have a fascination with the people you meet, don't just ask them generic questions about their demographics (work, nationality, marital status) but ask them questions about their passion and vision, ask them what they think and what they feel, ask them about what drives and motivates them. These sorts of questions open up far more interesting answers.

Additionally, these lines of enquiry don't just apply to strangers, they apply to those closest to you. Love is a journey, not a destination. There is always more learning and development in a relationship. When I interviewed my Dad about his life, I found out many things I didn't know. I gained extra clarity on things I hadn't fully understood, and received further nuggets of wisdom. Every time I listen back to that interview, I *still* gain something new from it. Now if asking my Dad questions can continue to develop our relationship after he's gone, imagine what it can do for the relationships you have with people who are still here.

Lavish

I believe love is something you find by giving it away. I think that is why left-brain thinkers struggle a little more with love, they can't understand this equation! Joking aside, it is a paradox that we need to wrap our heads around. In our society there is a mindset and culture that we only do things if there is something in it for us: we give gifts with the expectation of receiving them back, we do our job because we get paid, we buy someone a drink or take them out for dinner because we want to have sex with them (This is the Win/Lose mentality we talked about in the gratitude chapter).

Well here's a mindset shift: what about giving gifts because you love adding something to people's lives? What about doing work because of a love of serving people? What about enjoying giving oral sex because you make someone you love feel good?

We can cultivate love through consistent acts of giving. And when it comes to equations, the universe also likes equilibriums. When you give, you always receive. The key, however, is that you do not always receive from the source you gave it to. Thus when most people give a gift/favour/compliment, and don't receive something back, they get disheartened and don't bother anymore. Love is not a direct swap. It is a complex transaction. We must learn to feel the inherent joy in giving, and experience the benefit in the process, not the outcome. With that in mind, let's look at a couple of techniques for giving to others.

The first technique is to practice something that Brendon Burchard calls "Positive Projection". Instead of seeing the worst in people, we try to see the best in them. If you want someone to be a better person, try to see that better person in them. Try to see the aspects of them that you can reach an understanding and appreciation with.

But Positive Projection is more than just seeing the best in someone. It is called Positive *Projection* for a reason. We don't just want to see the best in someone, we want to *project* it on to them. You see we have mirror neurons in our brain, which copy and respond to what we see and feel around us. I'm sure many of you have a friend who you just can't help but feel happy around. They bound into the room and they're laughing and joking. Your mirror neurons kick in and your physiology begins to shift. Suddenly you feel upbeat and lively don't you?

An easy way to practice Positive Projection is to try and give praise at every opportunity. Receiving praise obviously activates some feel-good chemicals in our brain, but these same compounds are also activated though the act of *giving* praise. Our old friend oxytocin is pumped out, as well as another neurotransmitter called vasopressin, which research suggests plays a role in the bonding process. In close interactions, such as parent-child or sibling-sibling, vasopressin levels seem to be higher. Deficiencies in these neurotransmitters means a deficiency in connection, and thus in love.

The second way to lavish is to provide service. There are two ways to provide service: being meaningful, and creating meaning. Firstly, let's look at being meaningful. I'm talking about giving your inner resources to the world. You can give a lot to the world just by operating from your highest self. When you supply a skill for someone, you are being meaningful. When you inspire someone with one of your strengths, you are being meaningful. When you convey yourself with pure authenticity, you are being meaningful.

It goes back to our earlier discussion of being attractive. Why do you think someone falls in love with you romantically? They fall in love with what makes you the person you are. They fall in love with the qualities and attributes you express. Through being meaningful and giving these qualities and attributes, you are giving them love, and opening yourself up to receiving it.

The second way to provide service is to create meaning. This involves operating from your inner values as we outlined above, but it is directly changing the lives of others on a larger scale. Volunteering is being meaningful, founding a charity is creating meaning. It is an extra step in forming a long-lasting change. You are sending out love to the world on a larger scale. You are seeking to not influence one person at a time, but multiple people. When you look back on your life and ask what you achieved, it is how you created meaning that you will rank highest in your criteria of whether you lived a fulfilled life.

This was the final lesson I learned from my Dad's death. I learned there is more to love that what we give person to person. There is something greater than that. Love is what we leave in the world after we are gone. For my Dad, he left it with me, he left it with the close members of the family. But he could've left it with so many more people.

One of my strongest take-aways from my interview with Dad was when I asked him what he thought his greatest achievement in life was. His answer was: "Sometimes I feel like I haven't achieved that much really." This really struck me. My Dad had given a lot to me, but he didn't feel he had made an impact in the world. He hadn't created meaning in the way that he could've.

If I could summarise why Dad's death was such a game-changer for me, that would be it. Dad died without fulfilling his potential. He gave me love and service, and for that I am hugely grateful, but he had more to give. More people could've benefited from his knowledge and wisdom.

I realised that even more important than what we give to others, is what we give to the world. That is the highest form of love. It is connecting to the consciousness that unites us all. It is making a meaningful contribution to that shared consciousness. Because that contribution will outlast the years we spend in the living plane.

Questions and Activities

1. **The reason I am not opening myself up fully to love is…**

2. **I am worthy of love because…**

3. **The person/s I need to forgive is/are…**

4. **The person I should listen to more is…**

5. **I can be of more service by…**

6. **Pick two people to communicate to more deeply over the next 7 days. Evaluate how you feel after those 7 days.**

Chapter 6: Life after Death

How do you feel now?

We've covered a lot in the last three chapters. I respect there was a lot to take in there; numerous concepts to wrap your head around and many techniques and strategies to implement. I want to put you at ease by first saying you don't have to make all those changes in one shot.

Personal growth is an incremental process. In our society we are shown the overnight success, but you see, success doesn't happen overnight. *Publicity happens overnight.* The publicity comes as a snapshot of years and years of graft. But that's the part the media don't show us and people don't ask about.

I didn't write this book to be a one-hit pill of motivation. I wrote this as a resource. It is something you can refer back to as you continue to hone yourself.

Nonetheless, the immediate effect that I hope this book has achieved is that it has radically shifted your thinking. Maybe you were taking your life for granted. Maybe you weren't consciously designing the direction you wanted your life to go in. Maybe you didn't appreciate the components of existence that bring true fulfilment. I hope an immediate take-away you get from this book is that life is precious, you can't wander through it in a daze.

Let me share a bit of my inner nerd with you. As you may remember from an earlier chapter, I'm a massive Lord of the Rings fan. In the Lord of the Rings universe, the Valar (Gods) created two races: Elves and Men. Elves were immortal and perfect. Men were mortal and imperfect. Guess which race the Valar preferred?

The Men. You see Men appreciated their creation more. Because they were mortal, they saw the magic in every moment, because they would never be in that moment again. Because they were flawed, they were able to see the contrast in life, and thus appreciate the good and beautiful things in it so much more. I think many of us are walking through our lives thinking we're Elves, that we're immortal and perfect. Thus we never stop to appreciate the magic of our existence, and we never work on growing and improving ourselves. I hope that this book has made you realise, and also begin to appreciate, your mortality.

Perhaps you have been living with a lot of negativity. Statistically, it is fairly likely that you have suffered from one or both of anxiety or depression in your life. I bet you've felt burnout and stressed at some point. If you've been living life with the default setting stuck on "negative", I hope the chapter on gratitude will give you the means to shift that setting.

Gratitude is not a magic pill for these concerns, but it has shifted my consciousness in a phenomenal way. Since practicing gratitude, I have felt myself embrace a highly positive manner on a far more consistent basis. Through the regular practice of gratitude, you can alter your mindset in a pretty powerful way. The opportunity for gratitude is always there. Start searching for it, and you'll be amazed how often you find it.

Perhaps you haven't really been listening to your inner song. I'm sure you've worked in a few jobs you couldn't stand. I suspect you've had an existential crisis or two. Have you felt that for most of your life so far you've been living to a script that just isn't "you"? I hope the chapter on identity has helped you rewrite that script.

Expressing our identity doesn't get us to the destination, but it helps us know which is the right path to walk on. I spent much of my life trying to be something I wasn't, and there was a hole in me that I could never fully fill. Through working on self exploration and self expression I have felt a satisfaction within me that I have never felt before. When you walk along the path that is meant for you, there are some pretty awesome discoveries to make along the way. Work on yourself consistently, and you can enjoy some resounding successes.

Perhaps you've been living without love. I think you will have experienced at least one excruciatingly painful social rejection at some point in your life. I'm sure you have committed acts lacking in love. Have you felt your life has lacked meaning and connection? I hope the chapter on love has helped you find healing and solace.

It took losing love before I realised the value of it. Trying to love and appreciate every human I meet has shifted the connection I feel with life and the world around me. There is a whole lot of love out there to experience if you are willing to open yourself up to it. I now feel the higher meaning of my life, and you too can find this when you open yourself up to love.

In my work I dislike describing myself or being described as a "motivational speaker". Why is that? Because I don't want to motivate people, I want to transform them. I don't want to hype them up and leave them to it, I want to implement long lasting change in them. So what I don't want is for you to read this book, temporarily have some thoughts about life and death and go back to doing the same things that aren't bringing you happiness. I want you to really take heart of the lessons and perspective I've offered in this book, and use them to transform your life.

So the first thing I want you to do, if you haven't already, is to answer the questions I've provided at the end of each chapter. When you have (or if you have already) I want you to pick what you feel was the top insight from this exploration, and seek to implement that insight in your life. As I said, I'm not expecting you to integrate all my suggestions at once (I also don't expect you to integrate all of them anyway. Some will be suited to you, some may not), but I want you to start with one. Every journey starts with that first step, and if you don't take that first step after finishing this book, you will get limited value from reading it at all.

Now whilst I don't like the term "motivational speaker", I do want to share one last story. You remember my girlfriend/partner that I have mentioned throughout? You remember at the beginning of this book we walked together to my Dad's bedside. What I didn't tell you is that we had only been dating officially for a *week* when she sat with me as Dad passed.

Kerrie and I had known of each other for years, but my arrogance and insecurities had always kept her at a distance from me. Eventually we formed a very casual relationship just before I found out about my Dad's cancer. When I heard this news, I was vulnerable and exposed. All the barriers fell down. And this lady accepted me. She accepted everything that I had hidden behind the mask for so long. She showed incredible support and compassion for me, despite the fact that we weren't even properly dating.

When Dad was taken into hospital, I couldn't bear the thought of making the three hour journey back home, by myself, to watch my Dad withering away in his final days. Of all the people I had in my life, I wanted Kerrie there with me. It was then I realised how important this lady had become to me. With just 12 hours notice, she dropped everything to be at my side when I visited Dad. She was there by my side at his deathbed a week later. She was with me again at his funeral.

I had never experienced such unconditional love before, and it changed me. Every day she helps me work towards my highest self. She opened up the best parts of me that I hid away for too long. She's there to wipe away my tears when I'm struggling. She reminds me that I'm working on something greater than myself.

I tell you this to illustrate that I believe the universe made a deal with me. It took away someone I loved. It had lessons to teach me, and this was the only way in which I could learn them. But the universe likes balance. It really is a case of Yin and Yang. At the same time as I lost one special person, it brought another special person into my life. It tested me. If I could learn the lessons from Dad's death; if I worked hard on myself as a person; if I started to really live a life of love and service, then this girl would be there to share the journey with me. She would not have stayed with me if I had gone back to my old ways. I had to go through this moment of critical mass in order to find myself, connect with my mission, and find my life partner.

Everything we go through we go through for a very specific reason. If we can learn the lesson, then the universe rewards us. I was exceptionally fortunate that my trade occurred almost simultaneously, but what I can attest is that the trade will happen. Life is full of opposing energy: Masculine/Feminine, Day/Night, Happiness/Sadness, Triumph/Loss. The theme of this book has been Life and Death. I needed the death of my Dad to fully appreciate the joys of life. I needed that moment of Death to set in motion a number of forces that would lead me to experiencing more of Life.

What I would say to you is, if a 22-year-old in the depths of grief can find a way to create a better life for himself, you can too. There is nothing special about me. There is nothing that I have done that others can't. I have just worked hard and consistently. I have embraced the learning and growth that life has given me. Here I am just a year later writing my third book, running my own business, and getting to share it all with the woman I love. This change is possible for you too. But you need to realise how important your life is. You need to recognise that anything you want to happen you need to consciously design. The universe provides help when it sees that you have committed to making yourself and the world around you a whole lot better.

One of my Dad's mantras for life was "What would happen if everyone did it?". It was a mantra that he had taken from his Dad, and he tried to base all his moral and ethical decisions on this mantra. I hope to continue to pass this down the McCrae family. I repeat this mantra to you: "What would happen if everyone did it?". What would happen if everyone was a little more positive? What would happen if everyone was living their truth? What would happen if everyone showed more love to each other? It would be a much nicer world to live in: if you need any motivation for the decisions you make after finishing this book, I think that is it.

A Moment of Gratitude

One of the things I am consistently grateful for is the awesome people I have in my life. Whether that be my teachers, my friends or my students, I am inspired by so many people.

I'd first like to thank the two special ladies in my life, my partner Kerrie and my mum Sarah. Both are incredibly brave and tough, and have supported me through so many hard times.

Thank you Brendon Burchard, who I hope someday I will have the pleasure to meet personally. Spending four days at your *Experts Academy* Seminar changed my life. It give me so much belief and confidence for what I could achieve. Those four days inspired me to be a speaker, because I wanted to change people's lives the way you changed mine.

Thank you to my other virtual coaches and gurus: Tim Ferriss, Brian Johnson, Tony Robbins, Neil Strauss. Your work has helped me grow and develop so much over the last 18 months. Also a special shoutout to the teachers who are sadly no longer with us, Stephen Covey and Wayne Dyer. I hope I can help to continue your great work.

Thank you to the coaches who have helped me on my journey, notably Lauren Robertson, Ehab Hamarneh and Bob Train. I'd like to thank each of you for the richness of your belief in me and the support you were able to provide. I'm a young man with a lot to learn, but each of you have helped me learn faster.

Thank you to my oldest and dearest friends: Josh, Andy (x2), Jamie (x2), Ruairidh, Jonny, David, Thomas, Michael, Owen, Ben, Blair, and Nathan. We've had some great times together, and it's been an exciting time growing up with you all.

Thank you to the proofreaders of this book: Josh, Georgina, Ben, Jamie C, Andy, Ally, Jamie W, Aron, Isla, Suraya, Ely, Megan and John. Your feedback was encouraging, and reaffirmed my belief that this book could make a difference to people's lives.

A final thank you to YOU, the reader. If you've read this far then you have completed my whole book. You have listened to my story and I hope been impacted by my message. I wish you well in your future endeavours, and perhaps I will have the opportunity to meet you in the future.

If you've enjoyed this book, would you mind leaving me a rating and review on Amazon? Positive and negative feedback are both welcomed. You can also continue to follow me on Social Media. I'm "David McCrae: Personal Development Trainer" on Facebook, Youtube and Instagram.

In Love and Service,
David

The Last 60 Minutes
David McCrae
ISBN: 9781520277738

35361731R00054

Printed in Poland
by Amazon Fulfillment
Poland Sp. z o.o., Wrocław